W9-CKM-492

DISCARD

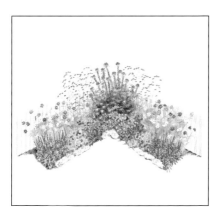

Dreamscaping

Library of Congress Cataloging-in-
Publication Data
Country living gardener dreamscaping:
25 easy designs for home gardens / by
the editors of Country living gardener.
        p. cm.
ISBN 1-58816-067-X
1. Gardens--Design.
I. Title: Country living gardener.
II. Country living gardener.
SB473 .C676 2001
712'.6--dc21
2001016928

For Country Living Gardener:
Diana Gold Murphy, Editor-in-Chief
Ruth Rogers Clausen, Horticulture Editor
Kathryn Drury, Managing Editor
Printed in Hong Kong

FIRST EDITION
1 2 3 4 5 6 7 8 9 10

Produced by
Blue Steel Communications,
Brooklyn, NY

Editor: Chris Peterson
Designer: Ray Leaning
Photo Editor: Ede Rothaus

www.cl-gardener.com

Dreamscaping

Ruth Rogers Clausen

25 Easy Designs for
Home Gardens

HEARST BOOKS
New York

USDA Plant Hardiness Zone Map

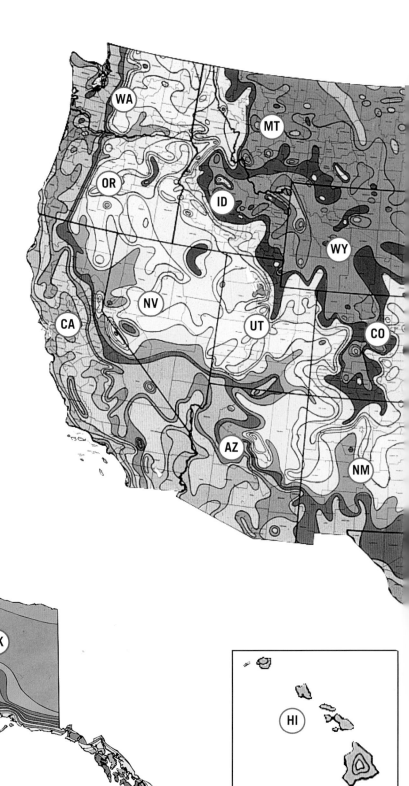

This map divides the U.S. into areas where winter low temperatures are the same within a few degrees. Use it as a guide to choosing plants that should survive the winter in your area. If a plant is hardy to Zone 5, this means it is hardy to -20°F, the average annual minimum temperature in Zone 5. The zones are approximate, so some gardeners experiment by growing plants rated hardy for one zone colder or warmer than their location. Hardiness zones don't indicate a plant's tolerance for heat, humidity, or any other factors that will affect its performance in your site.

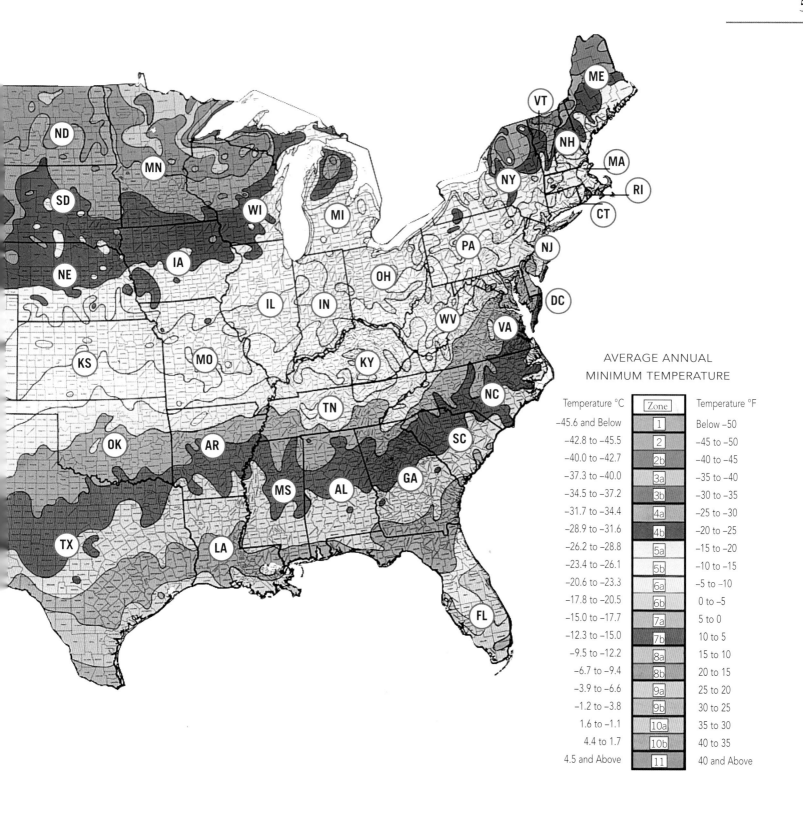

AVERAGE ANNUAL
MINIMUM TEMPERATURE

Temperature °C	Zone	Temperature °F
−45.6 and Below	1	Below −50
−42.8 to −45.5	2	−45 to −50
−40.0 to −42.7	2b	−40 to −45
−37.3 to −40.0	3a	−35 to −40
−34.5 to −37.2	3b	−30 to −35
−31.7 to −34.4	4a	−25 to −30
−28.9 to −31.6	4b	−20 to −25
−26.2 to −28.8	5a	−15 to −20
−23.4 to −26.1	5b	−10 to −15
−20.6 to −23.3	6a	−5 to −10
−17.8 to −20.5	6b	0 to −5
−15.0 to −17.7	7a	5 to 0
−12.3 to −15.0	7b	10 to 5
−9.5 to −12.2	8a	15 to 10
−6.7 to −9.4	8b	20 to 15
−3.9 to −6.6	9a	25 to 20
−1.2 to −3.8	9b	30 to 25
1.6 to −1.1	10a	35 to 30
4.4 to 1.7	10b	40 to 35
4.5 and Above	11	40 and Above

For all the gardeners and would-be gardeners who dream of having their own personal patch of Eden.

Many thanks to the staff of *Country Living Gardener*, especially Diana Murphy, Editor-in-Chief, and Betty Rice, Editorial Director of Hearst Books. Also thanks to Chris Peterson for keeping this project on track. I would like to take this opportunity to thank all my family, friends, and gardening colleagues who through the years have continued to inspire and educate me in the art and science of gardening.

Contents

Foreword 9
Introduction 11

Modest Marvels
12

Grand Schemes
50

Stunning Containers
88

Foreword

O ne of the most creative aspects of gardening is starting a new bed from scratch. There are so many factors to consider, including where to site it, how big it will be, and what shape it will take. Perhaps most important is the style; composing a garden is, after all, an artistic process much like painting on a blank canvas. You can fashion a relaxed cottage garden with flowers that are perfect for cutting, or a more formal, monochromatic design. No matter what size space you have—a tiny windowsill or a grand front entryway—this collection of plans by Ruth Rogers Clausen will take the guesswork out of turning a plain spot into a dramatic display. Ruth devised each plan to be easy to follow and simple to complete in a weekend or less. She's used plants that are widely available and suitable for a broad range of climates, and tackled different challenges in and around a home. Of course not every plan will be exactly right for your situation, and the plant selection may fall out of your particular zone. But the most engaging part of gardening is the fine-tuning, so feel free to adjust these plans to suit your needs and aesthetic whims. We've included a Design Alternatives section with suggested substitutions, but encourage you to experiment with your favorite plants and create a garden that is uniquely your own. Just have fun while enjoying each step of the process.

Diana Gold Murphy
Editor-in-Chief
Country Living Gardener

Introduction

Most of the gardens we admire in books or photographs have one thing in common: they all have some kind of structure or "bones," be it a path, an archway framing a view, a specimen plant as a focal point in the center or at the end of a path, or some other decorative feature. Even the smallest yard looks better with a little organization. This book is filled with plans for spaces of all sizes. You will find suggestions and ideas to help you make the most of what you have. Even if you don't follow the plan exactly, I hope that you will be inspired and encouraged to lay out your garden and experiment with what pleases you. Remember that your garden is a reflection of your own personal taste, so start with one of the plans in this book and then put your own stamp on it. For example, you might have a wonderful piece of driftwood collected on a vacation years ago. Why not incorporate this as a piece of garden art to replace a birdbath or fountain as a focal point? Or you might have a favorite plant, a peony or rose handed down through your family. Don't hesitate to plant it, but think about where it would show off best, in the optimum growing conditions of sun or shade, and give it some compatible companions. Although a garden continues to grow and is never truly finished, the plans and alternate plant choices here should give you confidence to move ahead and make the garden of your dreams come true.

Modest Marvels

Y ou may lack space but that doesn't mean you have to settle for a garden that falls short of your expectations. Combining vibrant, attention-grabbing plants in interesting and unusual combinations allows you to create big excitement in small areas. The designs in this section take advantage of plants that offer big bang for the buck in the form of multiple seasons of interest, spectacular blooms, or other outstanding features. The idea is to use every square foot in the most exciting way possible, and to allow background elements such as privacy fences or hedges to act as foils for the design. Remember, dynamite comes in small packages, and so do explosive garden designs.

- FULL SUN
- REGULAR WATERING
- SUMMER

creating your design

1 Dig up a bed 2' in from the fence, removing large rocks and other debris as you go. Sow California poppy seeds 4 to 6 weeks after the last frost; later, thin the seedlings to 6" apart.

2 In late spring, sow sweet alyssum seeds in 3 groups along the front edge of the design; thin the seedlings to 4" to 6" apart.

3 Plant 3 spider flowers 18" apart in a triangle at the back of the border.

4 Plant 2 groups of 3 verbenas, spacing seedlings 9" apart. Plant 2 groups of 3 cosmos each, leaving 12" to 15" between plants.

A Fence in Full Bloom

A fence can be so much more than a mere marker between where your property stops and the world beyond begins. A fence line, like so many areas in your yard, can serve as a backdrop for a stunning tableau of garden color. The narrow bed shown here has been designed for the full-sun exposure common to most fence areas. Anchored in a corner, the legs of the design can easily be repeated to run the length of a fence. The plants here were chosen for long bloom times and a diversity of flower shapes and colors, and they will thrive where the soil is average or even poor. In fact, avoid a heavy hand in applying fertilizer —overly rich soil encourages leafy growth at the expense of flowers. This is a fairly low-maintenance design as well; just apply a layer of organic mulch to discourage weeds and help retain moisture, and deadhead regularly to maintain a neat appearance and extend bloom time. As an added bonus, most of these make wonderful cut flowers for indoor bouquets. Substitute different annuals from year to year for a varied show of blooms along your fence.

5 Plant 2 arcs of 5 flowering tobaccos each; space the plants 9" apart.

6 Plant the mealy-cup sage in 2 groups of 7, leaving 9" between plants. Water the design well.

dollarwise

Buying healthy seedlings is one way to ensure bountiful blooms along your fence and to guard against money lost on plants that die shortly after planting. Beware of transplants that are too leggy (long stems), are rootbound, or whose foliage is turning yellow or brown. The chances are good that these plants will be stunted or will not survive the season.

A Spider flower (*Cleome hassleriana* 'Violet Queen'). The 3'- to 4'-tall stems of this bushy self-seeder are topped with tussled, spidery, deep lavender flowerheads.

B California poppy (*Eschscholzia californica* Thai Silk series). A key foreground plant in this design, this California poppy will grow 8" to 10" tall, with incredibly stunning and unique, semi-double, fluted blooms in brilliant reds, pinks, oranges, golds, and yellows.

C Tall verbena (*Verbena bonariensis*). This self-seeder has stiff 3' to 4' stems topped with clusters of tiny purple flowers that attract butterflies. Pinch young plants to induce bushiness.

D Mealy-cup sage (*Salvia farinacea* 'Victoria'). Great for cutting or drying, the 15"- to 18"-tall spikes of this perennial are crowded with blue-purple flowers. The stems themselves are a paler purple, complementing the bushy, light green foliage.

E Cosmos (*Cosmos bipinnatus* Sea Shells mix). The feathery foliage of this 2'- to 3'-tall annual provides an airy backdrop to the fluted "seashell" daisy flowers.

F Flowering tobacco (*Nicotiana alata* Nicki hybrids). This perennial

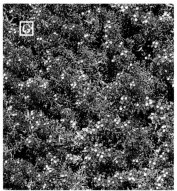

is treated as an annual in colder climates, and will grow 20" to 24". It provides fragrant, tubular, lime green, white, pink, or red flowers.

G Sweet alyssum (*Lobularia maritima* 'Rosie O'Day'). A useful and attractive wide-spreading edging plant, this 4"-tall, bushy annual offers a wealth of fragrant, rose-pink flowers.

inside info

Planting out seedlings of annuals is a simple process, but one that must be done correctly to give your plants the best possible start. Follow this basic five-step procedure to ensure your plants thrive in the design.

■ Plan to plant in the late afternoon after the heat of midday has passed and several hours after watering the plants; the soil should be moist.

■ Remove the plants from their pots or seed trays gently, disturbing the roots as little as possible; if they are in peat pots, tear the pots slightly to make it easy for the roots to grow through.

■ If the roots are compacted, loosen them gently before planting.

■ Dig a hole slightly larger than the rootball, and set the plant in at the same level at which it was growing in the trays or pots; peat pots must be completely buried.

■ Carefully firm the soil around the roots and water well after planting.

- ZONES 5-8
- SHADE
- LIGHT WATERING
- LATE SPRING

creating your design

1 Set out 3 rhododendrons and position 1 group of 3, and 1 group of 5 foxgloves, spacing plants 2' apart.

2 Consider how these plants will grow in. Once you're happy with their

placement, remove them from their containers and plant in holes slightly bigger than the containers.

3 Plant 1 group of 3 Bethlehem sage, and 1 group of 5 behind the bench,

Brilliant Color for a Shady Corner

Few places are as calming and restful as a peaceful hideaway in a shady corner of your garden or in a woodland setting of a larger garden. A quiet, shadowed alcove can provide a welcome contrast to fiery flowerbeds elsewhere, not to mention the allure of a place to escape your garden chores for a few minutes. This design was developed for a tree-shaded area that receives a fair amount of early sun. To reinforce the calm, restorative nature of the location while maintaining visual interest, the design combines bright colors with lush, variegated foliage in many shades of green. This makes the colors stand out, while softening the general look of the planting. Groups of the same plants have been repeated to bind the design together, which can easily be adapted for just about any garden. You can also choose any style of bench that suits your taste so long as it's durable, and will age with the design. Bring seasonal color to the bed by underplanting with fall-blooming perennials such as lilyturf, snakeroot, and Japanese anemones.

spacing plants 18" apart. Plant a line of 5 Solomon's seal 1' apart.

4 Plant 3 ferns singly, and position 3 astilbe 'Cattleya' 2' apart, next to the end of the bench, and 5 astilbe 'Bressingham Beauty' 2' apart.

5 Plant 3 barrenwort 1' apart, and 6 sweet woodruff in 2 groups of 3, allowing 1' between plants. Water the entire design well.

caution!

Use care when planting foxgloves; the flowers and foliage are poisonous. Choose a replacement or remove from the design if small children frequent the garden.

A Rosebay rhododendron (*Rhododendron maximum*). Zones 4-9. This shrub can grow 4ᶦ to 15ᶦ high. Large evergreen leaves provide a backdrop to trusses of bell-shaped rose, purplish pink, or white flowers that appear in late spring.

B Variegated Solomon's seal (*Polygonatum odoratum* 'Variegatum'). Zones 5-9. This understated perennial has white-margined leaves and fragrant white flowers on arched stems, to 18" tall.

C Astilbe (*Astilbe* x *arendsii* 'Cattleya'). Zones 4-8. This lovely perennial presents graceful panicles of rose pink flowers on 3ᶦ stems in early to mid summer, and sometimes again in early autumn.

D Astilbe (*Astilbe thunbergii* 'Bressingham Beauty'). Zones 4-8. Growing even taller than 'Cattleya', these plants produce fluffy panicles of bright pink flowers over gold-green foliage in mid summer.

E Barrenwort (*Epimedium* x *rubrum*). Zones 4-8. The spurred crimson and yellow flowers of this 1ᶦ

beauty dance above wiry-stemmed, heart-shaped leaves. The foliage turns red-brown in fall.

F Sweet woodruff (*Galium odoratum*). Zones 3-9. This charming groundcover only grows 9" tall, but offers fragrant, starry white flowers in late spring over whorls of emerald green leaves.

G Christmas fern (*Polystichum acrostichoides*). Zones 3-8. The evergreen fronds of this excellent native fern grow to about 18" tall,

spreading almost 3ᶦ wide.

H Bethlehem sage (*Pulmonaria saccharata* 'Mrs. Moon'). Zones 4-8. This tough groundcover has showy, silver-spotted green leaves, with tiny pink buds that open to attractive blue flowers in spring.

I White foxglove (*Digitalis purpurea* 'Alba'). Zones 4-8. This stunning biennial may grow over 4ᶦ high, with spikes of white bell-shaped flowers on erect stems, above a basal rosette of leaves.

Pest Control

Slugs can be a considerable problem in shady woodland areas, which tend to be consistently damp. If you have problems with slugs, consider one of these non-toxic deterrents:

▢ Sink several shallow containers (such as empty tuna or cat food cans) of flat beer in the soil. The slugs crawl in and drown—happy.

▢ Spread a barrier of fine grit or gravel around susceptible plants. When slugs try to attack, they quickly find they can't move over the sharp surface.

- ZONES 5-9
- FULL SUN
- REGULAR WATERING
- SPRING - FALL

Special Delivery

Ensure your address is the highlight of your mail carrier's route with a mailbox planting that will make delivering the post an occasion to stop and gawk. This is an excellent design for turning an unremarkable area into a showcase of garden color. Although it is essential that the space around your mailbox gets about five hours of sun, the other requirements are modest. Once planted, you'll need to do little maintenance beyond weeding and deadheading. Remember when siting your plants to leave space enough for the postal carrier to put mail in the box even when the plants are fully mature. You may even want to include a few paving stones to make the trip to the box a little easier. To get a jump on the spring blooms of this design, underplant the area with early-flowering blue squills, glory-of-the-snow, and small yellow narcissus such as a 'Peeping Tom' and 'Suzy.'

did you know?

Daylilies are more than a feast for the eye; they can serve in the kitchen too! Sauté the flowers with chive flowers and a little salt to make a wonderful side dish to chicken or meat courses.

creating your design

1 Use lime or sand to outline a wedge with the mailbox in the center. Dig the bed deeply, amending with plenty of compost.

2 Wrap the mailbox post with black mesh, providing a surface to which the clematis vines can cling. Plant 1 clematis on either side of the mailbox.

3 Plant 3 daylilies in a triangle around the mailbox, 15" apart. Plant the blue oat grass.

4 Plant a triangle of 3 veronicas, and an arc of 3 salvias, all 1' apart. Plant 3 pincushion flowers 9" to 12" apart.

5 Plant 2 thread-leaf coreopsis singly, at the outside corners, and 3 coreopsis 'Flying Saucers' 9" to 12" apart. Water the design well after planting.

A Thread-leaf tickseed (*Coreopsis verticillata* 'Zagreb'). Zones 3-10. This drought-resistant perennial covers itself with daisy-like yellow flowers summer through fall. The 12" to 15" stems bear abundant foliage.

B Daylily (*Hemerocallis* 'Black-Eyed Stella'). Zones 3-10. The grassy foliage of this long-blooming favorite acts as a foil for the funnel-shaped, yellow flowers with red throats. The stems grow from 18" to 24" tall.

C Sweet autumn clematis (*Clematis terniflora*). Zones 4-9. This climber blooms with billowy masses of 1" white flowers in late summer,

followed by silvery seedheads. The attractive deep green foliage lasts until first frost.

D Clematis (*Clematis* 'Multi Blue'). Zones 4-9. The frilly, double, 3" to 4", purplish-blue flowers of this vine set the stage in early summer for the sweet autumn clematis blooms to come. It may repeat bloom later.

E Pincushion flower (*Scabiosa columbaria* 'Butterfly blue'). Zones 5-10. The lilac-blue, 2" flowers of this evergreen perennial bloom in mid to late summer on 1' stems, over clumps of gray-green foliage.

F Blue oat grass (*Helictotrichon sempervirens*). Zones 4-9. This plant's 2'-tall clump of evergreen, blue-gray foliage is topped with arching buff flower spikes all summer.

G Sage (*Salvia* x *sylvestris* 'Blue Hill'). Zones 5-10. This durable perennial presents spikes of true blue flowers above sage green foliage from mid summer through early fall.

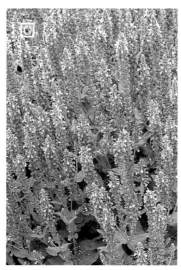

H Coreopsis (*Coreopsis* 'Flying Saucers'). Zones 4-9. Growing 18" to 24" tall, this plant produces abundant 2" to 3" golden-yellow daisy flowers from early summer through fall.

I Veronica (*Veronica* 'Goodness Grows'). Zones 4-9. The mailman will be delighted with these 1'-tall spikes of deep blue-purple flowers over mats of dusty gray green leaves.

design maintenance

Most of your aftercare efforts for this design will focus on the vines surrounding the mailbox.

☐ Mulch well with composted or rotted leaves around the roots of the clematis vines because they grow best when their "feet" are kept cool.

☐ In early spring, prune the sweet autumn clematis down to 1', and prune any straggly branches on the clematis "Multi Blue." If they grow too vigorously during the season, you may have to cut them back to allow access to the mailbox.

☐ During the season, routinely deadhead pincushion flower and coreopsis to extend bloom times. Deadhead the salvia and veronica at the base of the flower spikes.

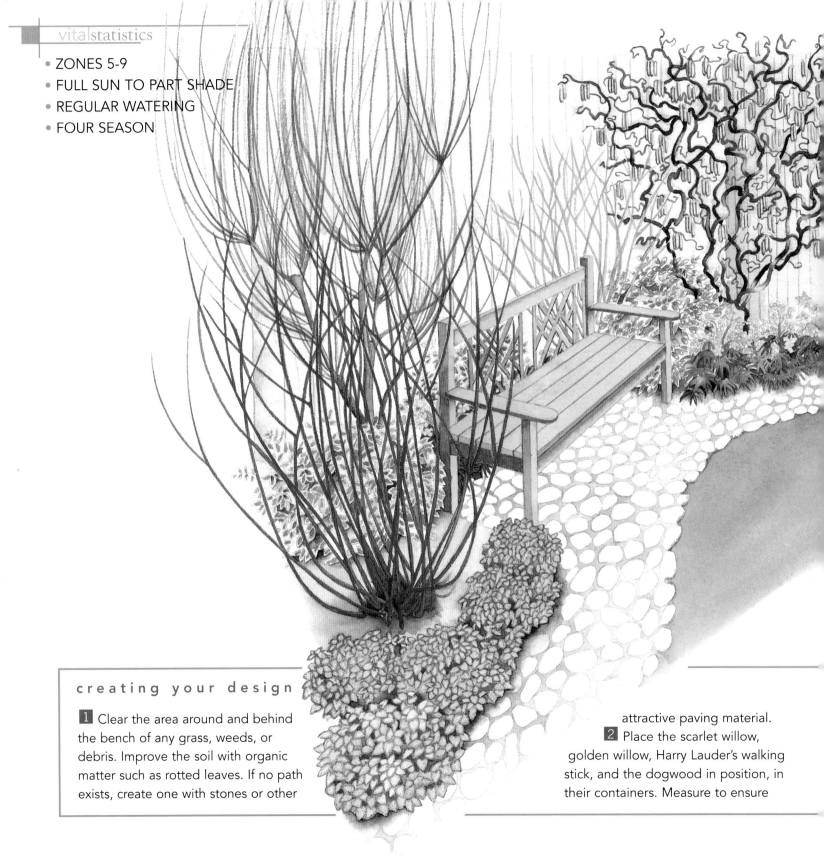

- ZONES 5-9
- FULL SUN TO PART SHADE
- REGULAR WATERING
- FOUR SEASON

creating your design

1 Clear the area around and behind the bench of any grass, weeds, or debris. Improve the soil with organic matter such as rotted leaves. If no path exists, create one with stones or other attractive paving material.

2 Place the scarlet willow, golden willow, Harry Lauder's walking stick, and the dogwood in position, in their containers. Measure to ensure

A Bounty of Bark Appeal

There's no reason for your garden to become dull and drab just because the cold weather has set in. Use a few carefully chosen and well-placed trees and shrubs to make the garden vibrant with colorful bark, evergreen foliage, and interesting growth habits. The design featured here is a fairly simple mix of trees—some grown as shrubs— and groundcovers. The serene sitting area they create serves as a wonderful winter alcove at the end of a garden, in a side yard, or overlooking a pond. This design has been placed inside a tall fence, although you can just as easily use high-growing hedges or a garden wall as a backdrop. Alternatively, the design can be situated in the 'el' of a house. The idea is to provide a cold-weather rest area sheltered from wind. Create a separation between the sitting area and the lawn with the paving stones shown here, or with alternatives such as pea gravel or even wood rounds. Even though the design is planned for winter interest, the plants are attractive year round. Supplement them with spring-flowering bulbs such as fiery red tulips, and summer-blooming annuals for long-term color.

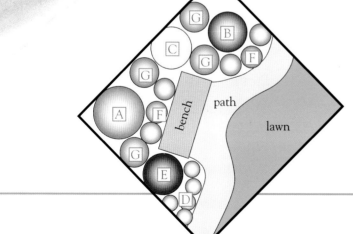

there is adequate room for growth between these plants, the fence and the bench.

3 Plant these trees and shrubs, then plant 3 wintercreepers, each equidistant between the trees.

4 Plant 2 groups of 3 setterworts, spacing plants 18" apart.

5 Plant 5 white deadnettles 15" apart. Water the bed thoroughly.

inside info

The branches of Harry Lauder's walking stick aren't just of interest in the garden. Prune the tree's twisted limbs for dramatic additions to indoor flower arrangements.

A Scarlet willow (*Salix alba* 'Britzensis'). Zones 4-9. For maximum impact, few trees can rival scarlet willow's upright stems covered with bright red bark. Male "pussy willow" catkins are followed by slender, bright green foliage.

B Harry Lauder's walking stick (*Corylus avellana* 'Contorta'). Zones 3-9. This distinctive tree is grown specifically for its madly twisted branches. Even the foliage is twisted, following male "lamb's tail" catkins.

C Golden willow (*Salix alba* 'Vitellina'). Zones 4-9. The bright, egg-yolk-colored stems make this tree a standout. Keep it pruned to shrub size for this design.

D White deadnettle (*Lamium maculatum* 'White Nancy'). Zones 3-10. This 10"-tall evergreen groundcover plant features silver leaves edged in green, and small white flowers in spring and, sporadically, later.

E Siberian dogwood (*Cornus alba* 'Sibirica'). Zones 2-8. Grown here as a shrub 6' to 7' tall, this tree offers bright red bark, especially on young stems, and red fall foliage color.

F Setterwort (*Helleborus foetidus*). Zones 3-10. In addition to its deeply fingered evergreen leaves, this 18"-tall perennial bears clusters of apple-green winter buds, and green flowers throughout the winter and spring. A poisonous plant, it self-sows freely.

G Wintercreeper (*Euonymus fortunei* 'Ivory Jade'). Zones 5-9. These plants provide a lovely underplanting to the design, growing to 2' tall, with a spreading habit. The rounded bright green foliage is edged with ivory and turns pink in cold weather.

design maintenance

The aftercare for this design is as much for aesthetics as it is for plant health. Because the groundcovers will largely prevent weeds, most aftercare will involve creative pruning of the trees.

■ Prune out a third of the older scarlet willow stems to the main branches each spring. This will force young growth with vibrant color. Train this tree as a standard and keep it pruned to 6' to 10' tall.

■ Prune a third of old golden willow and dogwood stems each year to encourage brighter colored new stems and to maintain a pleasing shape. Keep the golden willow pruned to shrub size.

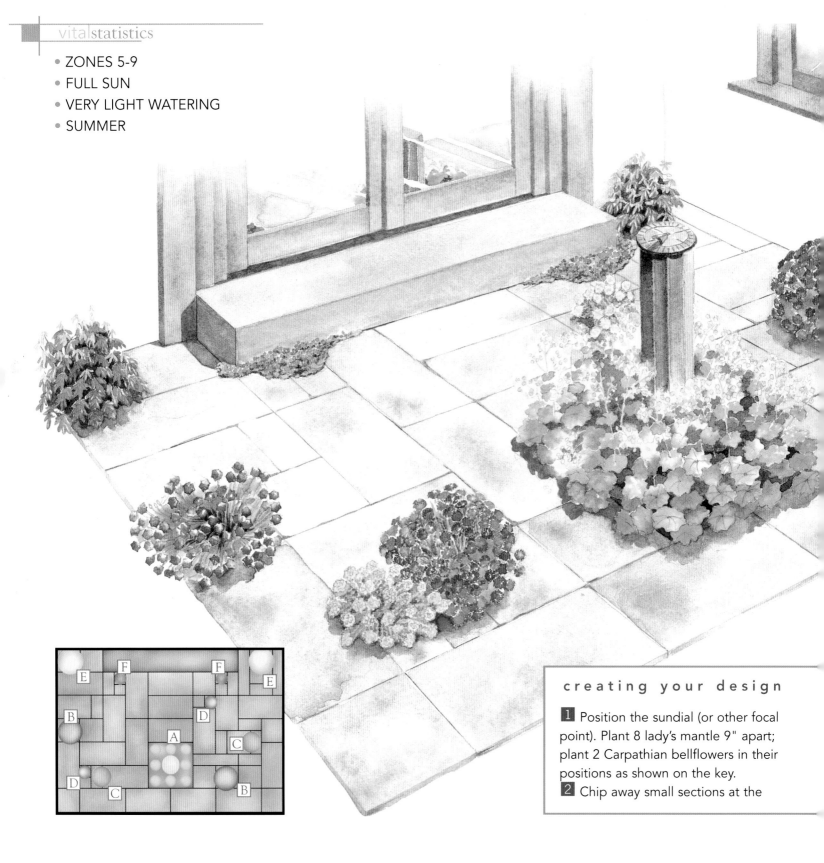

- ZONES 5-9
- FULL SUN
- VERY LIGHT WATERING
- SUMMER

creating your design

1 Position the sundial (or other focal point). Plant 8 lady's mantle 9" apart; plant 2 Carpathian bellflowers in their positions as shown on the key.

2 Chip away small sections at the

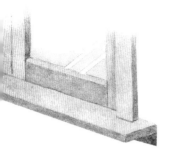

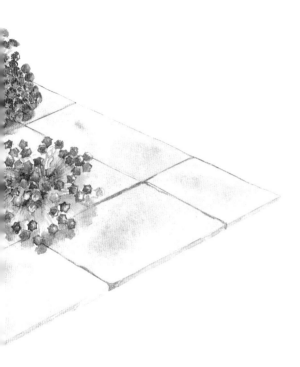

Splendor Among the Cracks

I f you need an innovative and unusual solution to liven up a dull patio, terrace, or shifting flagstone walk, a crevice garden may be just what you're looking for. Using a sundial, birdbath, or gazing ball stand as a focal point, and some compact flowering plants, you can create a dynamic garden design over a bare surface. Remove a few of your small patio pavers, chip corners off one or two, or dig up exposed areas where walkways have shifted to prepare for this unusual garden. Loosen the soil in these crevice areas and improve it with compost or other organic matter. This design uses a selection of low-growing, sprawling perennials; the species have been chosen for their attractive foliage for interest beyond their blooming season. Choose a site that receives good light and sun for five or more hours daily. Additional water is seldom required after the plants are established; allow them to grow naturally without extra fertilizer. Vary the design by planting groups of five to seven low-growing bulbs such as crocus, squills, or snowdrops for early spring color, or press seeds of compact annuals such as sweet alyssum, portulaca, and nemesia into the cracks for added summer pizzazz.

edges of the step, and plant 2 woolly thyme as shown.

3 Plant 2 cheddar pinks, 2 myrtle spurge, and 2 yellow corydalis singly, according to the key. Water the design well immediately after planting.

designguide

You can incorporate this design, or one like it, as part of the construction of a new patio or terrace. As with other garden projects, it's best to sketch the area and try out different compositions on paper before beginning the project. Although you can change the plants you use, you probably won't want to regularly change where pavers are placed.

green leaves. The deep-rose flowers carry a light fragrance. Deadhead for scattered rebloom.

D Myrtle spurge (*Euphorbia myrsinites*). Zones 5-10. A sprawling groundcover reaching 6" to 9" tall, myrtle spurge sends out stems clothed with whorls of blue-green leaves. In spring, yellow bracts surround inconspicuous flowers.

E Yellow corydalis (*Corydalis lutea*). Zones 5-10. This perennial has ferny leaves and brittle stems bearing abundant yellow flowers all season long. It grows 9" to 12" tall and self-seeds freely.

F Woolly thyme (*Thymus pseudolanuginosus*). Zones 5-10. The fragrant, 3"-tall mats of tiny, woolly, gray-green leaves on this herb are covered with attractive small spikes of rosy pink flowers in early summer. Woolly thyme will tolerate light foot traffic.

A Lady's mantle (*Alchemilla mollis*). Zones 3-9. This English garden favorite grows 12" to 15" tall, with rounded, hairy leaves, and sprays of chartreuse flowers in late spring.

B Carpathian bellflower (*Campanula carpatica* 'Blue Clips'). Zones 3-10. The toothed, heart-shaped leaves of this 8"- to 12"-tall perennial grow on trailing stems. It produces masses of 1"-wide, bright purple-blue flowers in spring.

C Cheddar pink (*Dianthus gratianopolitanus* 'Fire Witch'). Zones 5-10. This semi-evergreen forms 12"-tall rounded balls of grassy, blue-

- ZONES 5-7
- SUN TO PART SHADE
- FREQUENT WATERING
- FOUR SEASON

creating your design

1 Outline the informal curved front edge of the design with a garden hose. Dig out the edge and remove all grass, weeds, and rocks from the bed. Amend the soil with compost.

2 Plant the hydrangea and Japanese andromeda 5' to 6' apart. Plant the butterfly bush about 5' in front.

3 Plant 2 hollies in their respective positions. Allow 3' from the porch

edge to the plants.

4 Plant the sand cherry and 3 rhododendrons in position as shown on the key.

5 Plant 3 groups of 3 bleeding

Flowerful Foundation Planting

Shake loose the constraints of stuffy traditional foundation plantings, and dress up the front of a house or porch with this fabulous mixture of complementary trees, shrubs, and perennials. Where many more traditional foundation plantings feature rows of consistently sized shrubs with smaller, simple evergreens in the foreground, this design varies heights, spreads, and growing habits in an artful composition providing a wealth of visual interest. The range of blooms here will keep the bed vividly colorful from spring through late summer. The mix of shapes and the evergreen foliage types keep it looking good in the colder seasons. For early spring color, underplant throughout with groups of bulbs such as tulips, daffodils, crocuses, and squills. Add lively summer color by introducing long-blooming annuals such as petunias, verbena, heliotrope, and globe amaranth. For a bit of cottage garden atmosphere, train a climbing rose up the corner porch support.

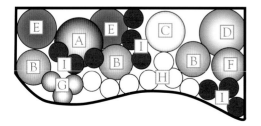

hearts, spacing the plants 15" apart.
6 Plant a group of 3 pincushion flowers, and a row of columbines, spacing all the plants 15" apart. Water the entire design thoroughly.

designguide

The visual arts rule of odd numbers applies to gardening: odd numbers of objects are visually appealing. If you use two of the same plant, use each singly in different areas.

(*Pieris japonica* 'Variegata'). Zones 5-8. At a mature height of 10′, this slow-growing evergreen may eventually tower over the design. Clusters of attractive greenish winter buds open to white lily-of-the-valley flowers in spring. The white-rimmed leaves are eye-catching year round.

E Inkberry holly (*Ilex glabra* 'Compacta'). Zones 5-9. This compact rounded shrub may reach 4′ to 6′ tall. Small evergreen leaves provide the background to tiny white flowers in early summer, with black berries in fall if the shrub is pollinated.

F Butterfly bush (*Buddleia davidii* 'Nanho Purple'). Zones 6-9. Silvery deciduous leaves complement the panicles of bright purple flowers that continue from mid summer until first frost on this bush.

G Pincushion flower (*Scabiosa columbaria* 'Butterfly Blue'). Zones 5-10. This clump-forming perennial sends up slender stems topped by lavender blue flowers 1" across, from spring to first frost.

H Columbine (*Aquilegia* hybrids). Zones 5-10. Dainty, long-spurred

A Purple-leaf sand cherry (*Prunus* x *cistena*). Zones 4-8. This tree-like deciduous shrub grows 7′ to 10′ tall, with strong, reddish purple foliage all season, and small, fragrant, pale pink flowers in mid spring. The purple-black berries that follow attract birds.

B Rhododendron (*Rhododendron*

yakushimanum). Zones 5-9. These shrubs grow into 3′-tall mounds of evergreen foliage, tan and wooly on the reverse. Rose-colored flowerbuds open to showy pink blooms in late spring.

C Oakleaf hydrangea (*Hydrangea quercifolia*). Zones 5-9. Forming a 4′

to 5′ rounded clump, this native shrub combines an attractive shape and bold deciduous foliage with intense red fall color. Large panicles of white flowers bloom in mid summer; exfoliating bark provides interest through winter.

D Variegated Japanese andromeda

flowers in pastel shades of pink, yellow, mauve, lavender, and white bloom on this delicate 2¹- to 3¹-tall perennial. The foliage provides a nice mid-green backdrop.

 Bleeding heart (*Dicentra*

spectabilis). Zones 3-10. The namesake pink-and-white heart-shaped flowers dangle from arching stems that reach 2¹ to 3¹ long. The attractive, slightly bluish foliage dies back when weather gets hot.

design maintenance

One of the nicest features about this design is the fact that although several different shrubs are included, the need for pruning is modest.

■ Prune the hollies only when they grow straggly branches, and only with hand pruners, never use a hedge trimmer.

■ Blooms appear on new wood on the butterfly bush, so prune hard in spring.

■ The sand cherry, Japanese andromeda, and hydrangea need no regular pruning. Prune for shape as necessary.

■ Be alert for unsightly white tracks on the foliage of the columbines, made by leaf miners. Pick off badly affected leaves and destroy.

- ZONES 5-8
- FULL SUN
- MODERATE WATERING
- SUMMER

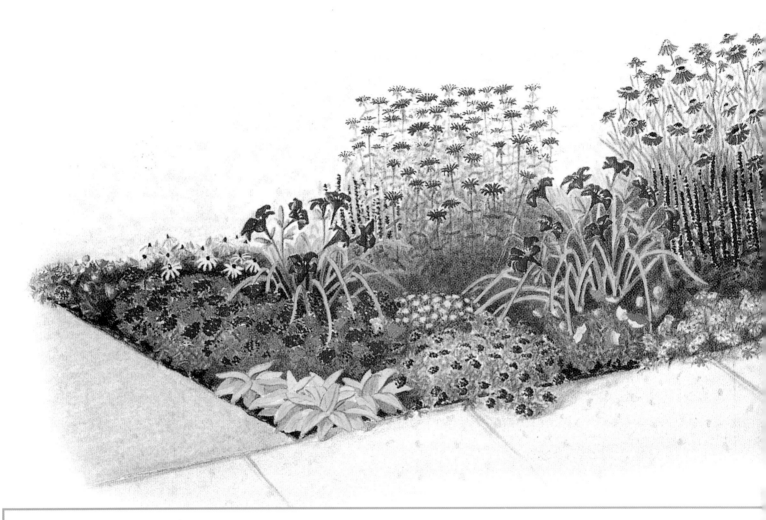

creating your design

1 Mark off a rectangular 6' x 10' bed, using stakes and string. Dig to the depth of a shovel blade and amend with well-rotted manure.

2 Plant 1 daylily 'James Marsh' and 3 beebalms spaced 15" apart; plant 1 group of 3 balloon flowers and 1 group of 8, spacing all plants 12" apart.

3 Edge with 2 groups of 5 Mexican zinnias, leaving 9" to 12" between plants. Plant 1 group of 5 hybrid sage and one group of 3 at the back, leaving 18" between plants.

4 Plant 5 daylily 'Stella d'Oro', 18" apart; plant 5 butterfly weed 18" apart. Plant 1 group of 3 black-eyed Susans and 1 group of 5, leaving about 18" between plants.

An Amazing Hot-Hued Bed

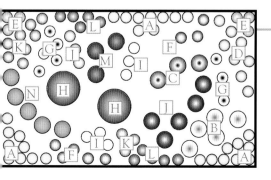

Few garden designs are as impressive as a walkaround bed bursting with hot-colored blooms that last from mid summer through early fall. The vibrant oranges, reds, and yellows of the basic color scheme here are intentionally contrasted with accents of blue-violet, and tempered by the cool silvery foliage of lamb's ears. The design is ideal for a variety of locations, from a sunny part of a lawn, to alongside a path or driveway. You can also repeat the design on any side to reshape or expand it as space permits. For the best growth and a wealth of blooms, ensure that the soil is rich in organic material to retain moisture, and plant in spring after danger of night frost has passed. Once established, they should need little extra water. The first season, before the perennials have filled out, tuck in more annuals—such as blue-violet mealy-cup sage 'Victoria' or orange calendulas and marigolds—as space permits. This is largely a carefree design, with little more than simple deadheading needed to keep the blooms coming right through Halloween.

5 Plant a swath of 5 veronicas 12" to 15" apart. Plant 2 groups of 3 'Zagreb', spacing them 12" apart; plant 3 sneezeweeds 18" apart. Plant 1 group of 5 and 1 group of 3 verbenas, spacing the plants 15" apart; and plant 3 groups of 9 lamb's ears, leaving 1' between plants.

6 Finish the design with 2 groups of 3 marigolds, spacing plants 6" to 8" apart. Water the entire design well and mulch to prevent weeds.

A Lamb's ears (*Stachys byzantina* 'Helene von Stein'). Zones 4-10. These 1' mats of furry silver foliage provide an excellent foil for the hotly colored blooms in this design.

B Daylily (*Hemerocallis* 'Stella d'Oro'). This bright yellow daylily presents blooms that are over 2"

wide, on stems more than 1' tall. It blooms repeatedly from early summer through fall.

C Sneezeweed (*Helenium* 'Moerheim Beauty'). Zones 3-10. The abundant flowers of this clump-forming perennial grow on 3' stems, presenting russet colors tinged with gold, summer through fall.

D Veronica (*Veronica* 'Sunny Border Blue'). Zones 4-8. Providing cool contrast, this perennial sends up stems 18" to 24" tall, topped with long spikes of deep purple flowers, mid summer through fall.

E French marigold (*Tagetes* 'Queen Sophia'). This bushy annual grows to 1' tall, with round, golden-yellow

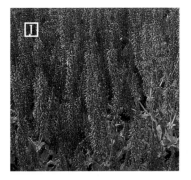

blooms summer through fall.
F Verbena (*Verbena* 'Homestead Purple'). Zones 5-10. This perennial features clusters of vibrant purple-pink blooms borne on long sprawling stems, accented by glossy green foliage. The flowers appear in early summer and continue into fall.
G Black-eyed Susan (*Rudbeckia fulgida* 'Goldsturm'). Zones 3-10. The distinctive, bright yellow daisy

blooms of this perennial are recognizable by their large black centers. The flowers appear summer through fall, growing on 2'-tall stems.
H Daylily (*Hemerocallis* 'James Marsh'). The strong red mid summer blooms of this daylily can hold their own even in this busy design. The stems grow 24" to 30".
I Thread-leaf tickseed (*Coreopsis verticillata* 'Zagreb'). Zones 3-10.

Brassy yellow-gold flowers cover these bushy 1' plants, summer to fall.
J Sage (*Salvia* x *sylvestris* 'May Night'). Zones 5-10. The indigo blue flower spikes of this perennial are set off by the wrinkled, hairy, mid green leaves. The plants grow 2' to 3' tall, with a spread of about 18".
K Balloon flower (*Platycodon grandiflorus* 'Mariesii'). Zones 3-10. Growing 12" to 18" tall, lovely cup-

shaped blue flowers open from delicate balloon-shaped buds in summer. This perennial is late to emerge in spring.
L Mexican zinnia (*Zinnia angustifolia* 'Golden Orange'). Dense clumps of foliage provide a base for the golden blooms on this self-cleaning plant. It grows up to 1' tall.
M Beebalm (*Monarda* 'Gardenview Scarlet'). Zones 4-10. The large clusters of scarlet flowers on this mid-summer perennial rise from 30" to 36" tall. The blooms attract bees and hummingbirds. The running roots may need to be restrained.
N Butterfly weed (*Asclepias tuberosa* 'Gay Butterflies'). Zones 3-10. This garden favorite attracts butterflies with its clusters of yellow, red, and orange flowers on 30" stems.

- ZONES 6-10
- FULL SUN
- REGULAR WATERING
- AUTUMN

creating your design

1 Clear the garden space and dig the bed up deeply. Position the 3 tuteurs in a triangle, with 2 in front.

2 Plant 3 'Baby Boo' pumpkin transplants, 1 on each side of a front tuteur. Repeat with 3 'Jack Be Little'.

3 Plant 3 gourds, 1 on each side of the rear tuteur. Plant 1 European cranberrybush, and 1 hydrangea. Plant the Japanese silver grass.

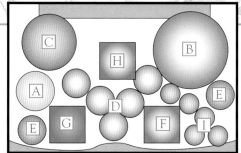

A Fall Decorating Garden

Tired of having to buy all the items you need to craft natural seasonal decorations? Use this design to grow your own bumper crop of unique decorative ornamentations. Although this bed is relatively small, the vertical nature of much of the growth ensures that you'll have all the decorative fruits you can handle. The design was developed with variety in mind, but if you're not a fan of white pumpkins or ornamental grasses, substitute seasonal variations that better suit your decorating needs. The design uses premade tuteurs available at most large garden centers, but it is easy to craft inexpensive substitutes out of bamboo canes or other sticks if you prefer. Some of the plants offer visual interest over the winter months; interplant with bulbs such as tulips and daffodils, and long-blooming annuals such as marigolds and zinnias, for color during spring and summer. Choose a site that gets good sun, where the soil is fertile, but not overly rich.

4 Plant 5 Chinese lanterns 18" apart; transplant 5 ornamental pepper seedlings, spacing them 12" apart. Plant 1 fountain grass at the left front corner, and 1 at the opposite edge.

insideinfo

For a little variety, you can change the color of your hydrangea blooms without changing the shrub. This is a wonderful experiment for children to try, not to mention a fun treat for adults. Just water the hydrangea with a simple solution of one teaspoon of alum (available in drugstores) mixed with one gallon of water. The new flowers will bloom purple.

A Japanese silver grass (*Miscanthus sinensis* 'Adagio'). Zones 4-9. The fluffy, silvery flower plumes of this ornamental grass rise 2' above the 3'-tall clump of fine grassy leaves that turn coppery in fall.

B European cranberrybush (*Viburnum opulus* 'Compactum'). Zones 4-8. This delightful deciduous shrub grows 4' to 6' tall and wide, with white flowers in spring and clusters of red berries in fall.

C Dwarf hydrangea (*Hydrangea macrophylla* 'Forever Pink'). Zones 6-9. Although smaller than its relatives, this deciduous shrub grows 2' to 3' and packs a wallop with its gorgeous, 4", candy-pink flower clusters, which fade and dry wonderfully.

D Chinese lantern plant (*Physalis alkekengi*). Zones 3-10. This unusual addition grows 1' to 2' tall, with bright orange, papery "lanterns" that contain the fruit. Although great for drying and use in swags, keep the plant in check because it may become invasive.

E Fountain grass (*Pennisetum alopecuroides* 'Hameln'). Zones 5-9. This compact 18"- to 24"-tall perennial grass sends up foxtail-like flower spikes above clumps of foliage that turn golden brown in autumn.

F Mini-pumpkin (*Cucurbita* 'Baby Boo'). This vine features ghostly white mini-pumpkins amidst profuse green foliage.

G Mini-pumpkin (*Cucurbita* 'Jack Be Little'). Similar to 'Baby Boo', this vine produces 3" bright yellow mini-pumpkins among dense foliage.

H Gourd (Small Fancy Gourds mix). Train transplants of this vine for a crop of dangling green, orange, yellow, and striped mini-gourds in assorted shapes and sizes.

I Ornamental pepper (*Capsicum annuum* 'Fiesta'). A marvelous little bush 12" to 15" tall and wide, this plant produces edible 2"-long fruits that mature from green, through yellow-orange to red.

design maintenance

The tuteurs in this design present a vertical dimension offering possibilities in other seasons, or during years you don't want to grow the pumpkins or other autumn vines.

For variation, try growing annual or perennial vines on one or more sides, leaving room for the pumpkin vines. Train clematis, honeysuckle, or a climbing rose up one side.

- FULL SUN
- HEAVY WATERING
- EARLY SPRING

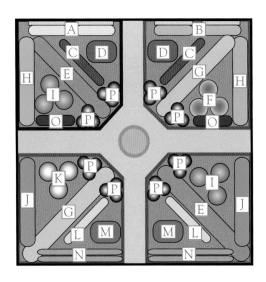

creating your design

1 Mark out the edges of the beds with landscaping ties, planks, or other edging that will contain the soil. Fill to the top with topsoil and compost mixed thoroughly. Install the trellises and supports.

2 Sow a row of snow pea seeds 1" apart in a band 4" to 6" wide. Sow a row of snap peas in the same way, as shown on the key.

3 Plant 8 groups of 3 violas, leaving 6" between plants; sow 2 diagonal rows of red-leaf lettuce seeds, spacing the seeds 1" apart. Sow rows of green-leaf lettuce in the same way. Thin as they are harvested.

4 Sow 2 rows of spinach seeds, spacing seeds 1" apart, and thinning

A Cool-Weather Formal Vegetable Garden

Who says vegetable gardens must necessarily be unruly, bland cousins to the beautiful flowerbeds in your garden? This design has arranged four productive raised beds in an attractive layout incorporating formal pathways and using a birdbath as a central focal point. Change the centerpiece to a sundial or another structure that suits your own aesthetic sense; mix and match the vegetables to appeal to your particular culinary preferences. All these plants have been chosen to thrive and produce before the heat of the summer months. To this end, the beds are raised to facilitate soil warming and provide an early start. After these crops are harvested, replace them with warm-weather vegetables, such as tomatoes, eggplants, and peppers. The design features bent-wood trellises for the peas to climb, but substitute other supports to suit your own garden style. You can also interplant with companion annuals such as marigolds, for added color and to help with pest control.

them to 2" to 3" apart. Do the same with Swiss chard seeds, thinning them to 10" apart.

5 Sow 2 groups of beet seeds 1" apart, thinning to 3" to 4" apart. Plant 3 broccoli transplants 12" to 15" apart, and 3 kale transplants 8" to 12" apart.

6 Sow 2 rows of fava bean seeds 4" to 6" apart; sow 2 rows of parsley seeds in a 2"-wide band, 10" apart. Sow 2 rows of carrot seeds about 1/4" apart, thinning to 3". Plant 3 cabbage transplants 12" to 15" apart, and a group of 3 broccoli transplants with the same spacing.

7 Sow clusters of mesclun seeds 1/2" apart; plant chives 8" apart in 2 rows along the front of the beds.

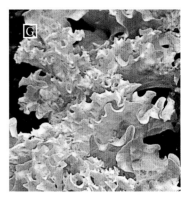

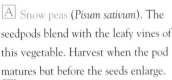

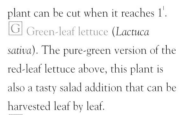

A Snow peas (*Pisum sativum*). The seedpods blend with the leafy vines of this vegetable. Harvest when the pod matures but before the seeds enlarge.

B Snap peas (*Pisum sativum*). These vines look much like snow peas, but the pods are thicker, and the peas are harvested when the pods are plump.

C Fava, or broad, beans (*Vicia faba*). This bushy, upright plant has blue-green foliage and thick pods with 3 to 4 seeds inside. Pick when young to use whole, or when mature to shell and eat as peas.

D Beets (*Beta vulgaris*). This root vegetable produces red stems and red-veined, 1'- tall leaves, as appealing in a mixed salad as the red beet itself.

E Red-leaf lettuce (*Lactuca sativa*). The mature, frilled, red-and-green mottled leaves of this plant can be harvested regularly through the season for fresh salads.

F Kale (*Brassica oleracea*). The rounded rosettes of green leaves can be harvested leaf by leaf when the leaves are about 3" long, or the whole plant can be cut when it reaches 1'.

G Green-leaf lettuce (*Lactuca sativa*). The pure-green version of the red-leaf lettuce above, this plant is also a tasty salad addition that can be harvested leaf by leaf.

H Spinach (*Brassica perviridis*). The bunches of broad, dark green leaves are usually harvested outside leaves first. Let the inner leaves mature before cutting, unless the plant begins to bolt (go to seed), than cut or pull the entire plant.

I Broccoli (*Brassica oleracea*). The central, light green flowerhead of this cancer-fighter is surrounded by large dark green leaves. Lateral heads mature later.

J Swiss chard (*Beta vulgaris*). A close relative of beets and spinach, this durable plant has edible stalks in bright red, orange, or green, with large, thick leaves.

K Cabbage (*Brassica oleracea*). The tight green head of this vegetable is wrapped in smooth, darker green leaves. Cut the head, but leave the stem and basal leaves, and you may get a second, smaller cabbage.

L Carrot (*Daucus carota*). Fine, ferny foliage on long, light green stems marks the location of these pumpkin-colored root vegetables.

M Mesclun. This is a seed mix

composed of several different leafy greens. It creates a salad in one spot that you should harvest frequently.

N Chives (*Allium schoenoprasum*). Zones 3-9. This onion relative has 1' tufts of grassy leaves. Use the pale purple flowers and green foliage to add flavor to your cooking.

O Parsley (*Petroselinum crispum*). The bright green curly leaves of this biennial rise 8" tall and are used in a range of main dishes and salads; they make excellent garnish.

P Violas (*Viola*). Zones 4-8. This mounding perennial is grown here as an annual for its edible purple flowers. It may self seed.

Grand Schemes

An impressive expanse calls for a big sweeping design statement. If you are fortunate enough to have significant outdoor space around your house, use it to create powerful designs that stay in the memory long after the season has faded. The layouts in this section were intended to fill maximum square footage with truly majestic beauty. They work well as part of a landscape with different and distinct sections, and generally include a wealth of species. Many of these schemes include interesting design elements that add to the planting, such as tuteurs, pathways, and birdbaths. If you dream big, look no further.

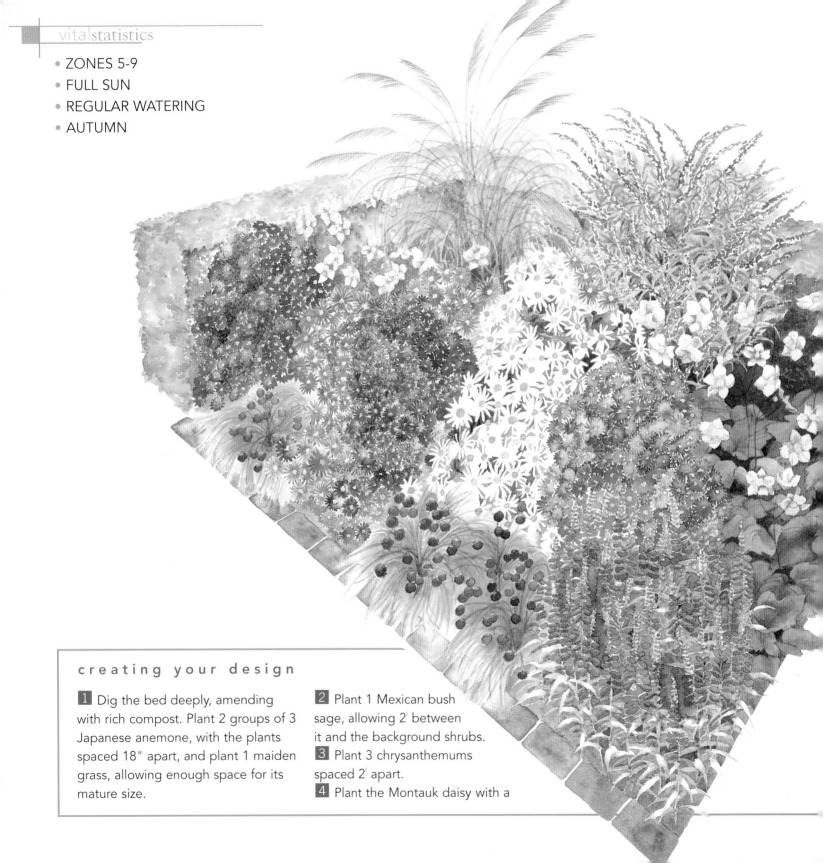

- ZONES 5-9
- FULL SUN
- REGULAR WATERING
- AUTUMN

creating your design

1 Dig the bed deeply, amending with rich compost. Plant 2 groups of 3 Japanese anemone, with the plants spaced 18" apart, and plant 1 maiden grass, allowing enough space for its mature size.

2 Plant 1 Mexican bush sage, allowing 2' between it and the background shrubs.

3 Plant 3 chrysanthemums spaced 2' apart.

4 Plant the Montauk daisy with a

Fabulous Fall Color Border

There's no reason to give up on bountiful blooms just because autumn has set in; this design provides a sensational blend of flower colors right up to the first frost, by combining an interesting selection of late-blooming perennials. The border here has been planted against a neat, 3' to 4' hedge of boxwood, but you can re-create the design against a row of other shrubs, a fence, or a stone wall. The goal is to provide a solid backdrop for the variety of flower colors. A 1'-wide "mowing strip" of pavers has been included along the front to keep the edge of the border neat and tidy. For a less formal look, you can use a hard plastic "invisible" edging strip. The design can be repeated if you have a longer space to fill. Regardless of where you site it, the border must have at least five hours of sun a day for optimal blooming and growth. The soil can be average, but should be amended with plenty of compost dug deeply to ensure good moisture retention. Add spring interest to the space by underplanting throughout with spring-blooming bulbs such as crocus, squills, narcissus, tulips, and hyacinths.

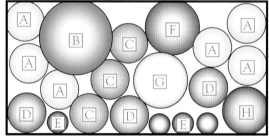

single aster 2' on either side, and 1 aster next to 'Clara Curtis'.
5 Plant the obedient plant, and plant 3 ornamental onions in a row, and 1 singly. Water well and apply leaf mulch around the plants.

designguide

The trick to keeping a garden interesting throughout the year is planning and planting for smooth transitions. To that end, spring-blooming bulbs are great complements to this design. Add groups of crocus and squills along the edges; the emerging perennials will camouflage the dying bulb foliage. Leave some extra space around plants to allow cutting flowers and weeding as needed.

A Japanese anemone (*Anemone hupehensis* 'September Charm'). Zones 6-10. Stunning 3", single, silvery pink flowers make this a charming addition to the design. This perennial grows up to 3¹ tall, with strong stems over

B Maiden grass (*Miscanthus sinensis* 'Morning Light'). Zones 4-9. This ornamental grass grows 4¹ to 6¹ tall, with finely textured arching leaves edged in white. In late summer, the mound of foliage is topped with reddish flower plumes that mature to silver and persist into winter.

C Chrysanthemum (*Chrysanthemum* 'Clara Curtis'). Zones 4-7. Attractive, deep pink daisy flowers cover this mounding 18" to 30" plant, and make long-lasting cut flowers.

D Aster (*Aster novae-angliae* 'Purple

mounds of dark foliage. An excellent cut flower.

Dome'). Zones 4-9. This prolific bloomer will fill in the design with mounds rising 2¹ to 4¹ tall, covered in semi-double, deep purple flowers.

E Ornamental onion (*Allium thunbergii* 'Ozawa'). Zones 4-9. Reddish-violet flowerheads on 8" to 10" stems rise above clumps of slender grassy leaves on this herb. The pretty blooms dry and retain their color for many weeks.

F Mexican bush sage (*Salvia leucantha*). Zones 7-10. This tender perennial should be treated as an annual north of zone 7. Mounds of grey-green leaves are topped with

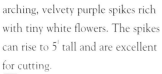

arching, velvety purple spikes rich with tiny white flowers. The spikes can rise to 5' tall and are excellent for cutting.

G Montauk daisy (*Nipponanthemum nipponicum*). Zones 6-10. Growing to over 2' tall, this plant features large white daisies above shrubby mounds of dark green leaves. Cut it back hard in spring as growth commences.

H Obedient plant (*Physostegia virginiana* 'Vivid'). Zones 3-10. The 2'-tall, upright spikes of vibrant rose-pink flowers on this perennial are long blooming and are excellent for cutting.

design maintenance

You can keep this border shapely by routinely cutting blooms for indoor display. Most of the regular aftercare is long term in nature.

■ Pinch the shoots of 'Clara Curtis' back by a third no later than July 4, to promote strong, bushy growth.

■ Divide the obedient plant, chrysanthemums, and asters every 2 to 3 years to keep these plants as vigorous as possible.

■ Where seasons are long, cut the Montauk daisy back by half to one-third in late June, to promote bushiness.

- ZONES 5-9
- FULL SUN
- REGULAR WATERING
- SPRING - SUMMER

creating your design

1 Dig up turf on either side of a pathway, leaving a grass strip 3' wide. Position the arch, ensuring that is securely fixed into the ground. Plant 1 *Rosa* 'Climbing Iceberg' and 1 clematis on one side of the trellis, and

1 *Rosa* 'William Baffin' and 1 clematis on the other side.

2 Position the roses in their containers to ensure that you are leaving enough room for deadheading and air circulation. Plant

A Rainbow of Roses and Friends

The ongoing romance with roses continues from generation to generation, and most dreamscapes would surely include at least a few roses. But the queen of flowers is twice as appealing when partnered with complementary perennials. The roses and perennials in this design were selected for their overlapping bloom times, as well as the attractive mix of plant and flower shapes and sizes. The garden will seem to change almost daily, offering a refreshing perspective any time you visit. For best results, select an open site that receives six or more hours of sun. Make sure that there is good air movement to deter the diseases that often plague roses. Roses are thirsty plants, so prepare the soil with plenty of organic matter for good drainage without drying out too rapidly, and be sure to keep the soil moist in times of drought. For added excitement, underplant with spring bulbs and cool-weather biennials such as pansies, and interplant with tall verbena and pink, white, or purple cleome for summer color at the rear on both sides.

1 each of 'Buff Beauty', 'Ballerina', 'Belinda', 'Mary Rose', 'Cornelia', and 'Yvonne Rabier'.

3 Plant 2 groups of 3 catmints each, spacing plants 30" apart; plant 3 groups of 7 foxgloves each, spacing plants 9" apart.

4 Plant 2 groups of 3 and 1 group of 5 milky bellflowers, spacing plants 2' apart; plant 2 groups of 5 and 1 group of 3 masterworts, leaving 1' between plants.

5 Finish by planting 2 groups of 5, and 2 groups of 3 sedum, leaving 1' between plants. Water the entire design well. Watch for blackspot on the roses and cut and discard in the trash affected leaves and stems.

- ZONES 5-8
- FULL SUN
- REGULAR WATERING
- SPRING - SUMMER

creating your design

1 Prepare the soil thoroughly, digging in plenty of compost or other humus-rich amendment to improve soil fertility and drainage.

2 Plant 1 of each butterfly bush according to the key; plant 2 honeysuckles singly.

3 Plant 2 phlox 'David', 2 'Laura', and 1 'Starfire'; plant 1 tricolor sage.

4 Plant 3 groups of 7 love-in-a-mist, and 3 groups of 3 each of parsley and chives. Leave 9" between plants.

A Fairy Tale Cottage Garden

Few garden design themes are so evocative as the notion of a true cottage garden. Whether you draw from the memory of a real cottage garden created by an aunt or grandmother long ago, or carry a romantic vision of one, the cottage style is the gardener's epitome of charm. This re-creation of the classic integrates captivating old-time annuals and perennials, useful herbs, and delightful flowering shrubs. All produce a simple informal display that would be perfectly at home next to a cozy thatched-roof structure. The design here is contained within the borders of a white picket fence, but you can let your own garden grow unconfined if you don't want to put a fence around your yard. Site this garden where it will receive six or more hours of sun each day. Underplant with spring bulbs for early color, and place a favorite chair in a corner of the garden so that you can read among the blooms or just daydream in peace.

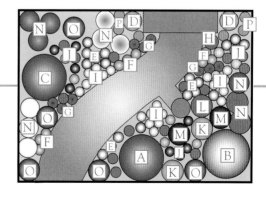

5 Plant 3 groups of 7 pot marigolds, spacing plants 9" apart; 4 groups of 3 hollyhocks, spacing plants 18" apart; and 2 groups of 3 morning glories, leaving 1' between the plants.
6 Plant 5 lavenders as indicated, water thoroughly, and mulch around plants to discourage weeds.

heckrottii). Zones 6-9. This woody vine may climb to 25' and offers clusters of very fragrant red-and-yellow flowers in summer.

E Love-in-a-mist (*Nigella damascena* Persian Jewels hybrids). This self-seeding annual grows 1' tall with saucer-shaped 1" flowers in white, pinks, and blues, above a ruff of threadlike leaves. The fruits are fat and inflated.

F Parsley (*Petroselinum crispum*). An indispensible culinary herb, parsley grows 1' tall with crisp, curly, bright green leaves. Harvest it regularly for best growth.

G Chives (*Allium schoenoprasum*). Zones 3-9. The round clusters of tiny purple flowers sit atop slender, onion-scented stems. Cut the leaves for flavoring and the spring-blooming flowerheads for garnish.

H Tricolor sage (*Salvia officinalis* 'Tricolor'). This herb grows 18" tall, with rough-textured, paddle-shaped, gray-green leaves splashed with pink and cream. It sends up spikes of blue flowers in late spring. Harvest the pungent leaves as needed for cooking.

I Pot marigold (*Calendula officinalis* Bon Bon hybrids). At 1' to 2' tall, this

compact annual produces double orange or yellow daisy flowers up to 4" across. The petals are edible.

J Larkspur (*Consolida ambigua*). Growing 1' to 3' tall, this annual sends up branching stems with spikes of pink, blue, or white flowers throughout the summer. The flowers are excellent for cutting.

K Garden phlox (*Phlox paniculata* 'David'). Zones 3-9. At 4' tall, this bushy perennial makes a real impact. Its large clusters of fragrant white flowers bloom in summer, and the foliage is mildew resistant.

L Garden phlox (*Phlox paniculata* 'Starfire'). Zones 3-9. The cherry red flowers on this 3'-tall perennial bloom in the summer.

M Garden phlox (*Phlox paniculata* 'Laura'). Zones 3-9. This phlox only

A Butterfly bush (*Buddleia davidii* 'Petite Indigo'). Zones 6-9. Narrow silvery leaves set off 3" to 4" spikes of pale violet flowers in summer and fall on this 5'-tall bush. The flowers attract butterflies.

B Butterfly bush (*Buddleia davidii* 'Pink Delight'). Zones 6-9. At 6' to 8' tall, this shrub is pruned as a tree for

this design. It bears 1'-long spikes of fragrant pink flowers in summer through fall.

C Butterfly bush (*Buddleia davidii* 'Nanho Purple'). Zones 6-9. Elegant spikes of lightly fragrant purple flowers in summer and fall set this bush apart. It grows 4' to 6'.

D Honeysuckle (*Lonicera* x

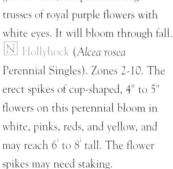

grows 3^l tall, but produces huge trusses of royal purple flowers with white eyes. It will bloom through fall.

N Hollyhock (*Alcea rosea* Perennial Singles). Zones 2-10. The erect spikes of cup-shaped, 4" to 5" flowers on this perennial bloom in white, pinks, reds, and yellow, and may reach 6^l to 8^l tall. The flower spikes may need staking.

O Lavender (*Lavandula angustifolia*).

Zones 5-8. Shrubby 3^l mounds of aromatic gray-green foliage support slender 8"-long spikes of fragrant blue violet flowers on this perennial. The flowers spikes are excellent for cutting and drying.

P Morning glory (*Ipomoea* 'Heavenly Blue'). This fast-growing annual vine will climb 9^l to 12^l tall, with sky blue trumpet flowers that open in the morning.

design maintenance

Cottage gardens need tending, but it is generally a pleasant chore, spent among a profusion of blooms and foliage.

☐ Deadhead regularly to keep the bed looking its best.

☐ Prune out old wood from the butterfly bushes in early spring. Prune 'Pink Delight' to

a single main trunk; in subsequent years prune old wood within the crown.

☐ Prune the honeysuckle regularly to keep it in bounds.

☐ Divide chives in early fall or spring.

☐ Prune the tricolor sage as needed to avoid legginess.

- ZONES 5-8
- FULL SUN
- REGULAR WATERING
- SPRING - SUMMER

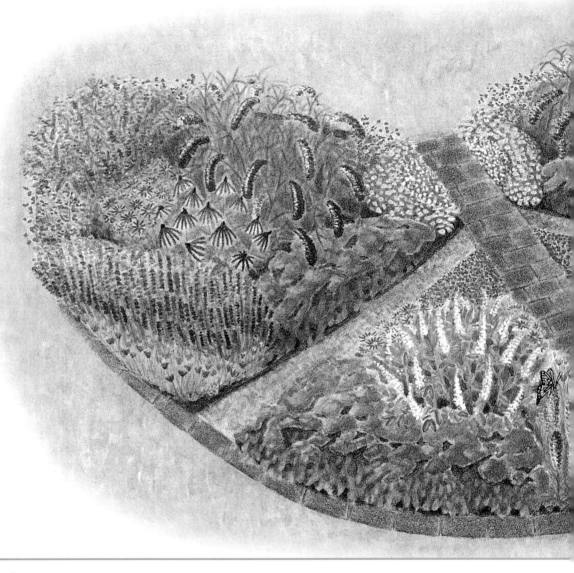

creating your design

1 Dig up the bed to the shape shown and amend the soil with compost. Prepare the outline with bricks, gravel, or other edging material, as you prefer.
2 Plant 1 of each butterfly bush on either side; plant 2 sweet

pepperbushes singly, as indicated.
3 Plant 12 asters in 4 groups of 3, allowing 20" between plants; set out 2 groups of 3 purple coneflowers, spacing plants 18" apart.
4 Plant 2 lavenders, 2' apart, on each

upper wing part. Plant 4 groups of 5 chives, leaving 1' between plants. Do the same with 20 cheddar pinks.
5 Plant 2 bluebeards and 2 rockcresses singly. Fill in with 2 groups of 7 coral bells, and 2 singles, spacing

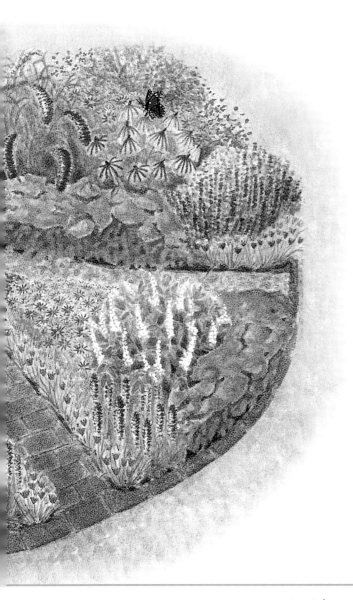

A Beautiful Butterfly Garden

Nothing makes a garden quite so magical as a cloud of butterflies fluttering over multi-colored flowers in the bright sun. The spectacular show of blooms created by this design not only supplies food for caterpillars and nectar for the hungry butterflies they become, it also provides an enjoyably long season of bloom. Although the design requires full sun, site it in a location shaded from wind, which can make it hard for butterflies to stop and feed. You'll also want to avoid chemical sprays of any sort to prevent poisoning the insects. Butterflies like to bask themselves on sun-warmed surfaces, so you'll help make them happy by placing out a few pieces of driftwood. Except for the shrubs, the spacing here is based on quart-sized plants. It may take a season for these perennials to fill in, offering the opportunity to tuck in annuals such as flowering tobacco, heliotrope, and verbena.

all 1' apart. Plant 16 stonecrops in 2 groups of 3 and 2 groups of 5, spacing plants 20" apart.

6 Plant 3 of each fleabane, spacing them 20" apart. Set out 2 groups of 3 dense blazing stars 18" apart.

insideinfo

If space allows at the top of this design, add a butterfly-shaped mud puddle filled with wet sand, which butterflies use as a source of mineral nutrients. Lay out some flat rocks on which butterflies can bask in the sun.

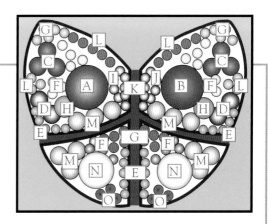

powder-blue flowers over aromatic gray-green leaves that are silvery underneath.

D Lavender (*Lavandula angustifolia* 'Munstead'). Zones 5-8. The aromatic gray foliage and purple flower spikes of this favorite low shrub grow to about 1'. The flower spikes are excellent for drying and are often included in potpourri.

E Chives (*Allium schoenoprasum*). Zones 3-9. This herb produces stems over 1' tall, topped with white or pale purple flowers. Both flowers and grassy foliage are edible, with an oniony flavor.

F Aster (*Aster x frikartii*). Zones 5-10. Growing 2' to 3' tall, the violet daisy-like blooms on this perennial appear from late spring through summer. A good cut flower.

G Cheddar pinks (*Dianthus gratianopolitanus*). Zones 5-10. At just 6" to 8" high, this flowering groundcover spreads nicely, with pink flowers over mats of grassy, gray-green foliage.

H Purple coneflower (*Echinacea purpurea* 'Magnus'). Zones 3-10. An excellent cut flower, this perennial

grows 3' stems topped with large purple daisy flowers, with orange-brown central cones.

I Hybrid fleabane (*Erigeron* 'Prosperity'). Zones 5-10. The double, mauve, daisy-like flowers of this mound-forming perennial have yellow centers and appear throughout summer; it grows 18" tall with the same spread.

J Hybrid fleabane (*Erigeron* 'Foerster's Darling'). Zones 3-10. This plant is essentially 'Prosperity', but with deep red-pink flowerheads on sturdy 18" stems.

K Rockcress (*Arabis caucasica*

A Butterfly bush (*Buddleia davidii* 'Petite Plum'). Zones 6-9. The deciduous gray foliage of this 4' bush serves as a foil for the arching panicles of red-purple flowers with orange eyes.

B Butterfly bush (*Buddleia davidii*

'Petite Purple'). Zones 6-9. With slightly more purple blooms, this shrub is a mirror to 'Petite Plum'.

C Bluebeard (*Caryopteris* x *clandonensis* 'Blue Mist'). Zones 6-9. This mound-forming shrub grows 2' to 3' tall, and features abundant

'Variegata'). Zones 4-10. Growing only 6" high, this mat-forming perennial groundcover bears variegated leaves with wide yellowish-white borders. The foliage is as interesting as the loose clusters of white flowers.

L Coral bells (*Heuchera* 'Firesprite'). Zones 4-10. Mounds of scalloped evergreen foliage support spikes of red flowers on 30" stems; they make great cut flowers.

M Stonecrop (*Sedum* 'Autumn Joy'). Zones 4-10. This bushy, clump-forming perennial grows 2' tall, with flat, brocolli-like heads of small star-shaped flowers that bloom deep pink and then become rust red, above small, gray-green succulent foliage.

N Sweet pepperbush (*Clethra alnifolia* 'Hummingbird'). Zones 3-9. This native bush may reach to 4', with short spikes of small, bell-shaped, fragrant white flowers in late summer and fall.

O Dense blazing star (*Liatris spicata* 'Kobold'). Zones 3-10. Liatris sends up 18" spikes of deep purple flowerheads summer to fall, over grassy, light green foliage.

- ZONES 4-7
- FULL SUN
- REGULAR WATERING
- SPRING

creating your design

1 In fall, before the ground freezes, dig the soil deeply, to a depth of 12" if possible, then plant the different groups of bulbs, as follows.

2 Plant 3 groups of 9 'February Gold' daffodils, 2 groups of 13 'Mount Hood' daffodils, and 1 group of 15 *Narcissus poeticus recurvus*, all about 8" deep and 6" apart in their groups.

3 Plant 1 group of 18 'Georgette' tulips 8" deep and 6" apart. Place 2 groups of 10 'Red Riding Hood' tulips and 2 groups of 10 'West Point' tulips, 6" deep and 6" apart.

4 Plant 2 groups of 3 crown imperial 4" deep, planting all the bulbs 18" apart.

5 Place 3 groups of 12 crocus corms

A Full Spring Bulb Show

I t's never too early to welcome spring to your garden! Using the right selection of bulbs, you can fill a bed with blooms to bid goodbye to frosty days. This design includes spring-flowering bulbs that begin blooming in zone 6 in early March, and keep the color coming through spring. To make the blooms pop out even more, the bed has been positioned against a low, evergreen hedge, such as yew or small-leaved holly. Although the optimal site is an open, sunny area, you can choose a location in light shade under deciduous trees; the trees will not leaf out until after the bulbs have finished blooming. The most important factor in choosing your site is to ensure that drainage is good; excess moisture can rot bulbs and ruin the display. If you prefer to camouflage the dying foliage, interplant the design with perennials such as astilbes, ferns, and hostas in light shade, and peonies and daylilies in full sun. If deer are a serious problem in your area, replace the tulips with more narcissus.

by type, all 3" apart; 2 groups of 12 snowdrops 12" apart; and 18 squills 5" apart. All should be 3" deep.

6 Cover with soil and firm—but don't compact—to make an even bed surface, water thoroughly, and mulch.

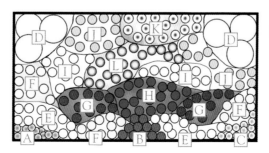

insideinfo

Early spring bulbs sometimes get tricked into a false start by an unseasonable warm spell. If substantial growth appears, protect the bulbs with a layer of compost or shredded leaves.

A Species crocus (*Crocus chrysanthus* 'Goldilocks'). This early bloomer offers small, rich golden goblets, several per corm.

B Species crocus (*Crocus chrysanthus* 'Lady Killer'). The striking dark purple flowers of this cultivar are edged in and open white, on 3" stems.

C Species crocus (*Crocus chrysanthus* 'Cream Beauty'). The flowers of this cultivar are a

sophisticated creamy white with delicate yellow throats.

D Crown imperial (*Fritillaria imperialis* 'Lutea'). These bulb flowers bloom just as the crocus flowers fade, presenting impressive clusters of yellow bells below tufts of foliage, on

2' to 3' stems. A unique addition to the design.

E Snowdrop (*Galanthus nivalis*). The snowdrop's early nodding white flowers bloom with the crocuses and grow 6" tall.

F Daffodil (*Narcissus* 'February

Gold'). Swept-back, bright yellow petals with darker yellow trumpets mark this early charmer. A good choice for forcing.

G Greigii tulip (*Tulipa greigii* 'Red Riding Hood'). The fire-engine red blooms of this 8"-tall tulip appear just

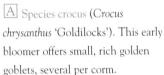

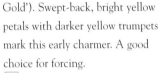

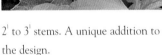

after the crocus blooms. The brown mottled leaves sustain interest for several weeks.

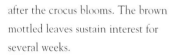 Siberian squill (*Scilla siberica* 'Spring Beauty'). Each 6" to 7" stem of this early bulb yields several nodding, brilliant blue flowers, in charming contrast to the snowdrops.

I Lily-flowered tulip (*Tulipa* 'West Point'). At 18" to 20" tall, these elegant tulips feature pointed petals of primrose yellow. They bloom as the 'Red Riding Hood' tulips fade.

J Daffodil (*Narcissus* 'Mount Hood'). White petals with cream trumpets set off this favorite 15"- to 17"-tall, heirloom daffodil.

K Daffodil (*Narcissus poeticus recurvus*). Growing 12" to 14" tall, this late-blooming beauty has white flowers with shallow, red-rimmed cups, and naturalizes well.

L Tulip (*Tulipa* 'Georgette'). This tulip has multiple yellow-edged red blooms on 18" to 20" stems. One of the last flowers to bloom in this garden, it is also one of the most impressively dramatic.

- ZONES 5-8
- PARTIAL SHADE
- LIGHT WATERING
- LATE WINTER

creating your design

1 In early fall, amend the soil well with organic material such as well-rotted compost, dug deeply. Dig a hole slightly larger than the witch hazel's rootball and plant the tree.

2 Leaving adequate room for their sizes when mature, plant 1 variegated Japanese andromeda and 1 Hinoki false cypress.

3 Plant 3 sweet box shrubs 2' apart, and 2 Lenten roses singly, as indicated on the key.

4 Plant 2 setterworts in their respective positions, and 3 bigroot geraniums 18" apart.

5 Divide 100 snowdrop bulbs into 3 groups and plant them randomly around the witch hazel, leaving 6"

A Fabulous Winterscape

Designing an interesting border for the cold winter months is one of the biggest challenges a gardener can face; this layout answers the challenge and then some. The trick to making a winter design work is choosing plants that provide interest in winter and beyond, and creating a layout that plays to the strength of each plant. The plants chosen here take up a sizable area, measuring about 15' by 8', but you can use fewer plants or substitute smaller shrubs to accommodate your own space constraints. However, try to maintain the same spacing relationship between plants as shown here. The design uses an intriguing interplay of deciduous and evergreen trees and shrubs, allowing for changes through seasons but avoiding the starkly bare appearance of many gardens in winter. When adapting the design to your own landscape, give careful consideration to how the plants will grow in—they'll be in place for a long time. For added interest, consider underplanting the witch hazel with an evergreen flowering groundcover such as *Lamium* 'Chequers' or 'White Nancy'.

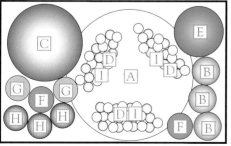

between bulbs; do the same with 100 winter aconites, planting them 3" apart among the snowdrops.

6 Water thoroughly and apply a generous layer of shredded pine bark or other organic mulch.

caution!

The Lenten rose and setterwort used in this design are poisonous plants. Consider substituting different small evergreen shrubs, or use more of the others in the design, if young children frequent the garden.

 Chinese witch hazel (*Hamamelis mollis*). Zones 5-9. This tree will grow 8' to 10' tall, but begins its 10' spread almost from the base. Gracefully twisting branches support very early, spidery yellow flowers that have a strong fragrance. The attractive deciduous foliage that follows turns bright yellow in fall.

B Sweet box (*Sarcococca hookerana var. humilis*). Zones 6-9. These dense, mounded shrubs provide insignificant but very fragrant white flowers in late winter. The lance-shaped evergreen foliage is interesting year round.

C Variegated Japanese andromeda (*Pieris japonica* 'Variegata'). Zones 6-9. Providing a stunning background to the Chinese witch hazel, this shrub will grow 10' tall, with a 5' spread. Slender sprays of winter buds open to white lily-of-the-valley flowers in spring. The evergreen foliage has a delicate white edging.

D Snowdrop (*Galanthus nivalis*). Zones 3-9. The nodding, pristine white flowers of this plant bloom on 6" stems in very early spring. The bulbs naturalize readily.

E Hinoki false cypress (*Chamaecyparis obtusa* 'Nana Gracilis'). Zones 5-9. Covered in dense, dark green foliage, this dwarf evergreen grows in a neat pyramid. Slow growing, it will eventually reach 5' to 6' tall, with a 3' to 4' spread.

F Lenten rose (*Helleborus orientalis*). Zones 3-10. The late-winter flowerbuds on this evergreen perennial open to cup-shaped, 2" pink or cream flowers, dappled inside with maroon. Its stems are topped with fingered leaves and can reach 2'.

G Setterwort (*Helleborus foetidus*). Zones 3-10. Reaching 18" to 2' tall, the long stout stems of this perennial support handsome fans of evergreen foliage and apple-green buds. The buds open in late winter, revealing maroon-rimmed bells.

H Bigroot geranium (*Geranium macrorrhizum*). Zones 4-8. Coppery in

winter, the 4"-wide, lobed leaves of this perennial have a pungent smell; clusters of elegant pink flowers bloom in late spring.

I Winter aconite (*Eranthis*

hyemalis). Zones 4-9. This 6" bulb displays lovely golden buttercups over light green ruffs in early spring. Soak the winter aconite's tuberous roots overnight prior to planting.

creating your design

1. Dig up the bed for planting and apply a light dressing of granular slow-release fertilizer, mixing it in well.

2. Position the butterfly bush in the center of the bed and plant; plant 8 lisianthus in 1 group of 5 and 1 group of 3; plant 5 cosmos. Leave 12" between all plants.

3. Plant 6 bells of Ireland in 2 groups of 3, and 5 tall verbena. Leave 12" between all plants.

4. Plant 5 mealy-cup sage 12" apart;

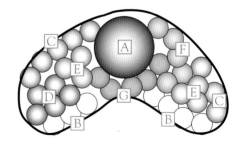

A Spectacular Cut-Flower Garden

Are you crazy for cut flowers but don't want to steal from your display beds and borders? This garden can be the perfect answer to your dilemma—a small area set aside just for flowers that you can cut for beautiful vase arrangements. The design doesn't need to take up a lot of space to produce a slew of bouquets; you can even tuck it into a corner near the vegetable garden, just so long as it is accessible. Leave room in back of the design for access to plants in the rear. The flowers selected will do best in full sun, planted in fertile, well-drained soil. Set the plants closer than normal for cutting purposes. Be sure to deadhead those flowers you don't cut, to keep the plants blooming their best and to maintain a tidy look overall. All the plants except the centerpiece butterfly bush are used as annuals; try out new cut-flower favorites each year for variety.

complete the design with 7 nasturtiums in 1 group of 4 and 1 group of 3, spacing plants 12" apart.

5 Water the planting thoroughly and apply a 2" to 3" layer of organic mulch to prevent weeds and retain moisture.

insideinfo

The trick to making the most of your cut flowers is ensuring that they can drink after they're cut. Early in the day, after the dew has dried, cut the flowers with sharp shears and immediately put them in cool water.

Recut them under lukewarm to cool water when you arrange them. Add a florist's mix to the water, or make your own with a teaspoon of sugar and a couple drops of liquid bleach (to kill stem-clogging bacteria).

A Butterfly bush (*Buddleia davidii* 'Nanho Blue'). Zones 6-9. This centerpiece shrub has deciduous gray foliage and grows 4' to 5' tall, with lilac-like spikes of mauve-blue flowers throughout summer. The flowers are fragrant and are very attractive to butterflies. Deadhead routinely for maximum bloom.

B Nasturtium (*Tropaeolum* 'Whirlybird Cream'). Creating an interesting edging, this annual features rounded leaves topped by semi-double, pale lemon flowers, all on a plant that grows 12" to 15" tall. Flowers, leaves, and seeds are edible.

C Lisianthus (*Eustoma* Double Eagle mix). This annual's impressive 2" semi-double flowers grow on stems 20" tall, in lavender, pink, and white, as well as bi-colors. The flowers are extremely long lasting.

D Mealy-cup sage (*Salvia farinacea* 'Victoria'). This annual bears 18"-tall spikes of violet-blue flowers over gray-green foliage. The flower spikes are excellent for drying.

E Bells of Ireland (*Moluccella laevis*). An unusual selection, this annual grows spikes of green, cup-like bracts surrounding tiny white flowers.

F Cosmos (*Cosmos* Sonata Series). Cosmos' long-lasting, 3"-wide blooms come in white, reds, and pinks, on stems up to 2' tall, over light green feathery foliage.

G Tall verbena (*Verbena bonariensis*). This tender perennial features strong, stiff 4' to 5' stems carrying 3" clusters of tiny purple flowers that attract butterflies.

design maintenance

This design requires little aftercare effort.

■ Mulch well to help prevent weeds.

■ Fertilize every two to three weeks with half-strength liquid fertilizer.

■ Deadhead routinely those faded blooms that you have not cut for bouquets.

- ZONES 4-8
- FULL SUN
- REGULAR WATERING
- SPRING - SUMMER

creating your design

1 Plant 3 perennial candytufts in their respective positions; plant 2 yellow corydalis according to the key.

2 Plant 3 dianthus, and 3 coral bells singly, as shown on the key. Plant 2 groups of 3 Dalmatian bellflowers,

spacing the plants 9" apart.

3 Plant 3 sea pinks 9" to 12" apart; and 2 basket-of-gold singly. Plant 3 mother-of-thyme 12" apart, and 1 singly, and plant 5 moss phlox in 5 positions according to the key.

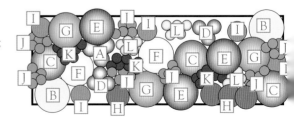

A Blooming Welcome

An awkward, narrow, front-yard strip is a landscaping challenge, but it can also be the opportunity to create a colorful, welcoming border. A multicolored show of blooms such as the one pictured here creates a tremendous first impression for visitors and passersby, increasing the "curb appeal" of your property. This particular design fills a 3' strip atop a retaining wall along a driveway. The design can easily be repeated to fill a longer space, such as the property edge of an elevated front yard. This planting includes a wide diversity of plants that were selected for their colorful display of blooms, and several are used to tumble over the edge of the wall, softening it. Although the plants thrive in average soil, they require good drainage. If your soil retains a lot of moisture, improve it with a significant amount of rotted compost or other organic material. Plant the bulbs in the fall, and overplant with annuals for summer color and variety. The illustration here shows the bed newly planted; the perennials will fill in as the season progresses.

insideinfo

4 In the fall, use a trowel or bulb tool to plant 7 groups of 5 Siberian squills 3" deep, 3 groups of 5 'Thalia' daffodils 6" to 8" deep, and 3 groups of Greigii tulips 5" to 6" deep, leaving 4" to 6" between all bulbs.

When planting bulbs among many other plants as in this design, a bulb planting tool makes the work go faster and easier. A step-on bulb planter is even better, allowing you to make many holes with less effort.

Always plant the bulbs and corms with the "nose"—the growing tip—pointed up toward the surface of the soil. If you are in doubt, ask your local nursery professional which end of the bulb is the growing tip.

A Sea pink, or thrift (*Armeria maritima*). Zones 3-10. The 1" heads of pink or white flowers on this perennial appear in late spring over dense 1' mounds of grassy, evergreen foliage. Thrift tolerates drought well.

B Basket-of-gold (*Aurinia saxatilis*). Zones 4-10. Clusters of fragrant, brilliant yellow flowers on 12" to 18" stems rise above the spreading clumps of gray-green leaves of this evergreen perennial.

C Perennial candytuft (*Iberis sempervirens*). Zones 3-10. Growing 1' tall, this subshrub develops evergreen mounds of dark foliage contrasting stunningly with the clusters of tiny pure white flowers spring through early summer.

D Dalmatian bellflower (*Campanula portenschlagiana*). Zones 5-10. At only 6" to 9" tall, this perennial offers clusters of bell-shaped purple-blue flowers in summer.

E Alpine pinks (*Dianthus alpinus*). Zones 4-10. This perennial features fringed white, pink, or red flowers, many with dark eyes, over loose clumps of evergreen, grassy, blue-green foliage.

F Yellow corydalis (*Corydalis lutea*). Zones 5-10. The delicate ferny leaves of this 12"- to 15"-tall perennial provide contrast to the yellow flowers that bloom from late spring until fall. It self sows freely.

G Coral bells (*Heuchera* 'Firefly'). Zones 4-10. This charming perennial has mounds of evergreen scalloped leaves below airy spikes of red flowers on 1' to 2' stems in spring through

summer. Other cultivars would work well here also.

H Mother-of-thyme (*Thymus serpyllum*). Zones 4-10. Low, spreading mats of the tiny evergreen leaves on this aromatic subshrub support clusters of tiny crimson to pale pink or white flowers on 4" stems, early summer through fall.

I Moss phlox (*Phlox subulata* 'Blue Emerald'). Zones 4-9. In spring, this 6"- to 9"-tall rock garden favorite has abundant lavender blue flowers over evergreen carpets of stiff, needle-like leaves.

J Siberian squill (*Scilla siberica*). Zones 5-8. Pendant, brilliant blue flowers on 6" stems appear in spring, from these fall-planted bulbs.

K Gregii tulip (*Tulipa greigii* 'Red Riding Hood'). Growing 10" tall, the crimson blooms of this tulip appear early. The brown mottled leaves provide interest for several weeks.

L Triandrus daffodil (*Narcissus* 'Thalia'). Each 12" to 14" stem of this bulb will hold two to three pure white trumpet flowers in spring. The pristine flowers carry a delicate fragrance.

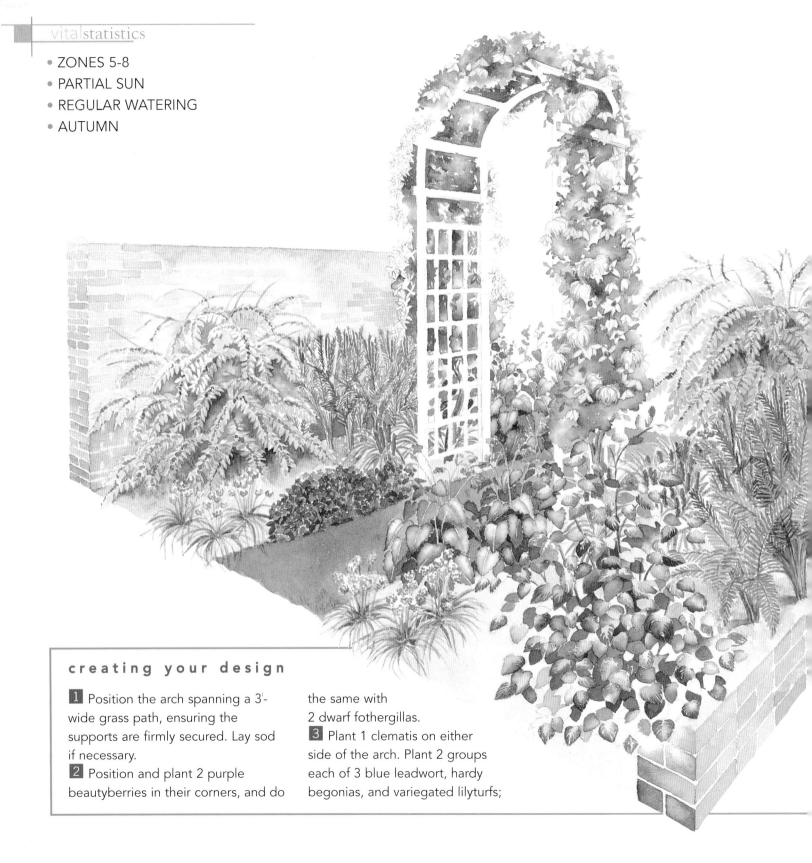

- ZONES 5-8
- PARTIAL SUN
- REGULAR WATERING
- AUTUMN

creating your design

1 Position the arch spanning a 3'-wide grass path, ensuring the supports are firmly secured. Lay sod if necessary.

2 Position and plant 2 purple beautyberries in their corners, and do the same with 2 dwarf fothergillas.

3 Plant 1 clematis on either side of the arch. Plant 2 groups each of 3 blue leadwort, hardy begonias, and variegated lilyturfs;

An Amazing Autumn Color Bed

G ive your garden a little zest after Labor Day by creating this wonderful mixed bed for fall. Using both vertical and horizontal elements, this design achieves maximum impact from a modest number of plants. The simple plan features low-maintenance perennials for lots of late-season interest without a great deal of effort. The beds shown here are backed by a 6' to 8' fence, wall, or hedge, and flank a neat grass path spanned by a small wooden arch. If you're not fond of mowing, substitute a gravel walk for the grass, or a different style of arch if you desire. Average soil and sun or part shade are fine for these plants. Add some interest in other seasons by underplanting with spring-blooming bulbs, such as early tulips or white and yellow daffodils. For stunning summer color amidst a wealth of foliage, tuck flowering annuals, such as zinnias, marigolds, coreopsis, wishbone flowers or cosmos, in between the shrubs and perennials.

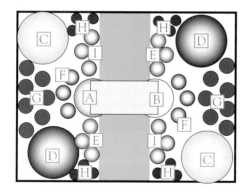

space all 15" to 18" apart.
4 Plant 4 groups of 3 ornamental onions, spacing the plants 12" to 15" apart; finish the design with 2 groups of 7 cinnamon ferns, spacing the ferns 18" to 24" apart.

insideinfo

Late autumn is the perfect time to clean up your garden in preparation for winter. Remove any dead plants and debris from the garden as soon as the plants die down, to avoid harboring pests and diseases over winter. In colder northern zones, bring garden hoses indoors so they won't crack. This is also a good time to clean and repair tools, such as hoes, shovels, and reel mowers, for storage over winter.

A Sweet autumn clematis (*Clematis terniflora*). Zones 4-9. This impressive vine can grow more than 25' and provides masses of delicate, fragrant white flowers in fall.

B Clematis (*Clematis orientalis*). Zones 6-9. Growing as large as C. *terniflora*, this vine bears waxy, bright yellow 1" flowers in late summer, followed by a profusion of attractive silver-tailed seed clusters.

C Dwarf fothergilla (*Fothergilla gardenii*). Zones 5-9. Fluffy white spring flowers precede impressive yellow and orange fall foliage on this 4'-tall, native, deciduous shrub.

D Purple beautyberry (*Callicarpa dichotoma*). Zones 6-9. This 4'- to 5'-tall deciduous shrub shines in fall with clusters of eye-catching violet berries along the stems.

E Blue leadwort (*Ceratostigma plumbaginoides*). Zones 5-10. The stems and bronze-green foliage of this 1'-tall groundcover turn dark red in cold weather. Its brilliant blue, funnel-shaped flowers bloom atop reddish bracts.

F Variegated lilyturf (*Liriope muscari* 'Variegata'). Zones 5-10. In autumn, this perennial has spikes of tiny purple flowers on stems to 15" tall. The 1/2"-wide, strap-shaped foliage is edged with yellow and remains attractive through winter.

G Cinnamon fern (*Osmunda cinnamomea*). Zones 4-8. This impressive fern grows 3' to 5' tall, with upright clumps of fronds that turn yellow and orange in the fall.

H Ornamental onion (*Allium thunbergii* 'Ozawa'). Zones 4-9. Late in the season, this underused perennial produces deep rose flowerheads on 1' stems, above clumps of grassy foliage.

I Hardy begonia (*Begonia grandis*). Zones 6-9. Showy clusters of pink flowers top arching cane-like stems on this 2' to 3' tuberous perennial. Bold angel-wing leaves hide a striking reddish reverse.

design maintenance

This design is largely care-free, with just a couple of simple tasks required.

■ Prune both of the clematis vines back to 2' above ground level every 2 to 3 years.

■ Prune the purple beautyberry in early spring; it blooms and fruits best on young wood.

■ At spring clean-up time, fertilize lightly with a balanced fertilizer and mulch with shredded leaves or compost.

Stunning Containers

Create a moveable, changeable visual feast by planting in containers. The designs in this section offer options that work in limited space or accent larger gardens. Container gardens allow you to control the culture of the plants, and to make quick and easy changes to suit your preferences or changing conditions. The range of designs presented here offer something for just about any season or location, from a sunny window in the kitchen, to a shaded, bare corner of the deck or patio. Your favorite plants captured in containers are like jewels in a setting, and provide spotlights for you to come back to again and again.

- ALL ZONES
- FULL SUN
- FREQUENT WATERING
- SUMMER

creating your design

1 Firmly attach your window box to the window ledge or wall, using galvanized steel brackets designed to support 30 to 50 pounds. Secure with 3" wood screws into wood siding, and anchor bolts into masonry.

A Brilliant Box of Blooms

Window boxes are as much about shape and texture as they are about color. The design here uses a mix of bushy, upright plants and sprawling trailers. The informal stems of the licorice plant and nasturtiums soften the edges of the box and provide visual support to the concentration of blooms on the other plants.

A south-facing windowsill is the perfect place for an impressive annual display. Window box gardens allow you the opportunity to create a stunning display of your favorite flowers to enjoy from inside or outside the house. This window box is filled with easy-to-grow annuals that flourish in direct sun and bloom with a riot of color throughout the summer, right into fall. Plant it after the danger of frost has passed, although the nasturtiums may be sown a few weeks earlier. Make sure that the window box you choose provides good drainage—waterlogged annuals will not bloom well. For variety, consider planting scented plants such as scented geraniums or trailing rosemary. Position the box on a sunny outside kitchen windowsill and you'll be able to reach out and cut nasturtium blooms for salads!

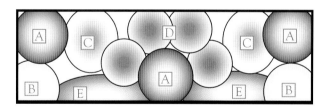

2 Cover the drainage holes with window screen and fill the box with sterilized soilless potting mix.
3 Direct sow 2 seeds of each nasturtium in position, and later thin out the smaller seedling of each pair.

4 Plant 3 cupflowers, and 4 marigolds in an arc, leaving 4" to 6" between seedlings.
5 Plant 2 licorice plants, and water the box well. Feed with half-strength liquid fertilizer every 2 to 3 weeks.

For maximum bushiness, pinch the young cupflower and marigold transplants. Avoid chemical pesticides and you'll be able to eat the peppery leaves and flowers of the nasturtiums.

A Cupflower (*Nierembergia hippomanica* var. *violacea* 'Purple Robe'). A free-blooming filler, this plant will grow to 8" in all directions, with bright purple flowers among ferny foliage.

B Nasturtium (*Tropaeolum majus* 'Moonlight'). The trailing stems of 'Moonlight' will grow to 3' long, bearing broad, pale yellow flowers with deeper yellow throats.

C Nasturtium (*Tropaeolum majus* 'Strawberries & Cream'). Yellow flowers blotched with red at the throat are borne on this sprawling plant that grows 10" to 12" tall and 9" across.

D Marigold (*Tagetes patula* 'Naughty Marietta'). This annual grows 9" tall with an 8" spread. Each single golden flower carries an eye-catching maroon blotch; the foliage is pleasantly pungent.

E Licorice plant (*Helichrysum petiolare*). This foliage filler has small felted silver leaves on stems to 3' long. It's good for threading through the other plants.

inside info

Window boxes should be checked regularly for structural integrity. Wet soil and creeping plant roots can weaken the joints of the box, and the supports can pull away from the surface to which they are attached. Check your box monthly and make repairs as necessary. If your window box is wooden, as in this design, repaint each year before planting new annuals.

- ALL ZONES
- FULL SUN
- LIGHT WATERING
- ALL SEASONS

Inside info

Whenever you need to move the pot, tip it and slide a piece of carpet remnant under it or use a container dolly. You can then slide the heavy pot wherever you want it to go without leaving scrape marks.

creating your design

1 Fill a 12-pocket terra cotta strawberry jar with a 1:1 mix of cactus potting soil—or some other free-draining soil mix—combined with compost, from the base up to the bottom row of pockets.

2 Tuck 2 hens-and-chicks and 2

A Shapely Succulent Collection

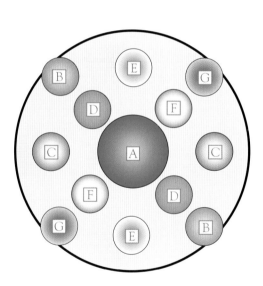

L ooking for an unusual and attention-getting focal point for your cool sunroom or garden this winter? Look no further. This decorative, large-pocket, terra cotta strawberry jar features an assortment of interesting succulents, chosen for their foliage color and textural contrasts. This design also illustrates the surprising variety of growing habits available among succulents, including plants that spread, trail, and grow upright. Select a sun-rich spot that gets bright light, and where the temperature does not fall below 45°F to 50°F. In warm-winter regions, use this addition to liven up a patio or terrace. In colder climates, keep it indoors near a sunny window and move it outdoors when the weather warms up. An especially maintenance-free container, the design is particularly adaptable; try out new cactus varieties or other specialty succulents for a range of colors and textures.

jellybean plants into 4 separate pockets, firming the soil around the plants; fill with soil mix to the next level of pockets.

3 Plant 2 string of beads and 2 burro's-tail stonecrop in 4 pockets, and gently tamp down the soil. Fill with soil to the top level of pockets.

4 Plant 2 pussy ears and 2 spider houseleeks alternating in the 4 top pockets. Position the jade tree and fill around it with soil mix. Firm the plants into place and keep them moist until they are established.

A Jade tree (*Crassula ovata*). Zones 9-10. An impressive centerpiece, this upright plant has branching fleshy stems bearing thick, rounded, jade-green leaves, often rimmed with red.

B Hens-and-chicks (*Sempervivum tectorum*). Zones 5-10. Complementing the jade tree, these plants feature sturdy 3" to 4" rosettes of pointed, red-tipped green leaves.

These will increase by offsets to create colonies.

C Burro's-tail stonecrop (*Sedum morganianum*). Zone 10. The pendant, rope-like stems of this plant have fleshy, cylindrical, whitish-green leaves, each about 1" long.

D Pussy ears (*Kalanchoe tomentosa*). Zone 10. This succulent has loose rosettes of 1¹/2" spoon-shaped leaves

with a white, felt-like covering, sometimes tipped with brown.

E String of beads (*Senecio rowleyanus*). The slender dangling stems crowded with 1/4", bright green, bead-like leaves provide an almost whimsical contrast to the stiff habits of the other plants in the design.

F Spider houseleek (*Sempervivum arachnoideum*). Zones 5-10. The dense

3/4" rosettes of pointed green leaves on this plant are covered with cobweb-like hairs. The offsets grow slowly, forming colonies.

G Jellybean plant (*Sedum rubrotinctum*). Zones 5-10. This plant offers 8"-tall mounds of lax stems, bearing close-set, pinkish-red, cylindrical leaves. The plant loses the red coloring in poor light.

design maintenance

One of the wonderful aspects of succulents is that they require very little water.

■ When the days are short in cooler months, water only once every six weeks. In hotter periods, once a month is sufficient.

■ Feed succulents twice a year. Each fall and spring scratch a sprinkling of a low-nitrogen, slow-release fertilizer into each pocket.

■ To maintain correct proportions, keep the jade tree pruned to about 12".

- ALL ZONES
- FULL SUN
- LIGHT WATERING
- WINTER

An Indoor Winter Herb Box

Y ou don't have to wait until late spring or summer to enjoy the simple pleasure of fresh herbs; you can have them year-round with this lush, indoor herb window box. This design includes popular culinary herbs that are ideal for overwintering on a bright, south-facing kitchen windowsill. The box shown here measures about 19" wide and 6" deep, but choose one that fits your own windowsill and adapt the design as needed. Depending on your décor, you can use a box made of wood, terra cotta, or plastic; just make sure that whatever container you pick has several drainage holes in the bottom. Herbs in 2" to 3" pots from your local nursery are best for this design, and the plants can be transplanted into your garden in spring.

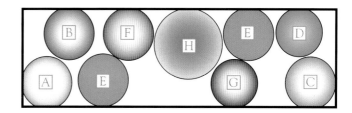

creating your design

1 Place sreening or coffee filters over the drainage holes in the box to limit soil loss; fill the box halfway with very well drained, all-purpose potting soil mix. Dampen the soil thoroughly.

2 Position the rosemary in the center of the box and plant 1 chives and 1 tricolor sage on either side of it; plant the other chives toward the front as shown on the key.

3 Plant both types of parsley, both of the thymes, and the purple sage. Fill to the top of the box with potting soil and firm around all of the plants.

4 Water the entire box well.

A Variegated lemon thyme (*Thymus* x *citriodorus* 'Silver Queen'). Zones 4-10. Rising 10" to 12" tall, this evergreen features tiny, strongly lemon-scented, gray-green leaves, attractively bordered with white.

B Flat-leaved, or Italian, parsley (*Petroselinum crispum*). Zones 5-8. The simple, flat, dark green leaves on the 8" to 1' stems of this biennial have a stronger flavor than the curly-leaved type.

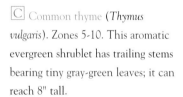

C Common thyme (*Thymus vulgaris*). Zones 5-10. This aromatic evergreen shrublet has trailing stems bearing tiny gray-green leaves; it can reach 8" tall.

D Curly-leaved parsley (*Petroselinum crispum*). Zones 5-8. This 8"-tall biennial has bright green curly leaves that are beautiful as a garnish. Combine them with thyme and bay for a *bouquet garni*.

E Chives (*Allium schoenoprasum*). Zones 3-9. The slender, pointed, dark green leaves of this perennial grow 12" to 15" tall. They have a mild onion flavor, and the edible flowerheads are attractive in salads.

F Tricolor sage (*Salvia officinalis* 'Tricolor'). Zones 5-10. This beautiful evergreen shrub can grow to 2' tall with 2"-long leaves variegated with cream, purple, and green. It delivers a strong flavor, excellent in stews,

stuffings, or for seasoning meat.

G Purple sage (*Salvia officinalis* 'Purpurea'). Zones 5-10. The young leaves of this evergreen shrub are dark purple, lightening with age. The foliage has a pungent odor.

H Rosemary (*Rosmarinus officinalis*). Zones 8-10. Over time, this evergreen shrub can grow to 4'. It has small pale blue or white flowers and needle-like, pine-scented leaves.

---

design maintenance

A few minor aftercare chores will keep your herb box yeilding a constant crop.

☐ Feed with half-strength liquid fertilizer once a month.

☐ Mist underneath the leaves daily to discourage pests such as white fly and red spider mites.

☐ Harvest the leaves frequently.

☐ Turn the window box around every couple of weeks to ensure even light and growth. If you prefer, you can fill the box with potted herbs to be planted out for the growing season.

- ALL ZONES
- FULL LIGHT
- LIGHT WATERING
- ALL SEASONS

creating your design

1 Place your mini-greenhouse in position, out of direct sun but in a brightly lit area. Fill the bottom tray with pea gravel.

2 Pot up 2 African violets, 2 Cape primroses, and 2 small-flowered Cape primroses, each in a 4" pot. Plant 6 miniature African violets in 2½" pots. Plant the florist's gloxinia in a 5" pot.

3 Position all the pots on the

A Glass House Festival of Flowers

Extend your gardening year-round with this wonderful indoor greenhouse. Whether you want to grow tropical plants that would not survive outside, or desire common garden favorites such as vegetables out of season, an indoor greenhouse is an ideal solution. The design here uses a mini-greenhouse that is 32" by 17" and just over 21" tall. This size allows you to grow a reasonable number of plants in a structure that is fairly easy to move. You can, however, find a range of sizes in catalogs. The plants used here all belong to the *Gesneriad* family and thrive in similar conditions: moderate temperatures, high humidity, and bright filtered light. To avoid overheating, position the greenhouse out of direct sun. Try to keep the temperature at about 65°F inside; if it gets too warm, open the side ventilators. Select cultivars in colors that appeal to you. After bloom time, the plants can remain in the greenhouse or be nurtured elsewhere—making way for another display of blooming or foliage plants.

greenhouse gravel tray. Reposition the pots as necessary for the most pleasing composition.

4 Water the gravel and all of the plants thoroughly.

designguide

Depending on what you choose to grow, an indoor greenhouse can serve a practical as well as aesthetic purpose. In winter, consider filling the greenhouse with your favorite salad makings, such as mesclun and radishes, for fresh produce during the colder months. Include edible flowers, such as nasturtiums, to keep the design as beautiful as it is useful.

[A] African violet (*Saintpaulia* hybrid cultivars). These delicate tropical plants offer stunning flowers in purples, pinks, and lavender, often with ruffled petals, over fuzzy, deep green foliage. They will spread nicely, to about 4" across, and grow about 2" above the height of the pot.

[B] Miniature African violet (*Saintpaulia* hybrid cultivars). These diminutive plants complement their larger relatives, featuring tiny blooms in showstopping pinks, whites, and purples, over fuzzy, dark green leaves.

[C] Cape primrose (*Streptocarpus* x *hybridus* cultivars). With their long, light green leaves and fuchsia, red, or light blue flowers on arching stems, these primroses offer interesting contrasting shapes to the other flowers in the greenhouse. They will grow 12" tall and wide.

[D] Cape primrose (*Streptocarpus* x *hybridus* small-flowered cultivars). These complement the larger primroses, featuring lots of small green leaves on sprawling stems that spread to about 12" and grow about 9" tall. The attractive dainty flowers bloom in lavender and blue over a very long period.

[E] Florist's gloxinia (*Sinningia speciosa* cultivars). Presenting dramatic purple or red flowers with white throats over large velvety leaves, this centerpiece plant can spread to 14" and grow 12" tall.

design maintenance

Proper watering is crucial for these plants.

☐ For the violets and gloxinia, keep the soil evenly moist, watering from below with a mix of tepid water and half-strength fertilizer.

☐ Allow the soil of the primroses to dry out between waterings and fertilize with half-strength fertilizer every two weeks.

☐ Keep the gravel bed moist to provide a constant source of humidity to all the plants in the greenhouse.

- FULL SUN
- NO WATERING
- SUMMER

caution!

Be careful not to substitute the plants in this design for invasive species, especially where they can overwinter. If you live in a warmer climate, avoid water hyacinths and water lettuce, both of which can spread beyond your garden and cause serious environmental damage.

creating your design

1 Buy a sturdy half whiskey barrel that sits steady on its base and is secured with tight metal hoops. Scrub inside and out thoroughly, and wire brush and repaint the hoops. Seal the inside or use a liner secured to the lip.

2 Drill a hole 1" below the rim to allow for overflow in rainy weather.

Eye-catching Water Garden

This small water garden captures the charm of a pond, but with a size and mobility that allows it to be placed in a residential garden, on a deck, terrace, or patio. A container water garden such as this is also an excellent addition to a small, Japanese-style garden, or just as an accent in a sunny corner of a larger garden. The beauty of this particular design is that it achieves maximum impact with a modest number of plants, requiring little effort and minimal expense. If you decide to place the barrel on a deck or other supported structure, be sure that the structure's supports can handle the weight of the barrel full of water. For variety year to year, consider one of the dozens of different small-size water lilies or lotuses, and you can even add koi or other pond fish. Just be sure to bring them inside for the winter months in colder regions.

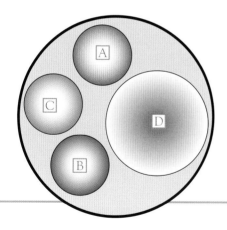

Place the barrel in its desired position before filling with water. Fill to well below final level, to allow for placement of the plant pots.

3 Fill a black plant pot with heavy garden soil rather than potting soil. Place the water lily rhizome, with cut side at the edge of the pot and the growing tip toward the center. Spread the roots, cover all except the growing tip with a thin layer of soil, and top with a layer of pea gravel. Position in the barrel on bricks, so that the roots sit 12" or less below the water surface.

4 Plant the Japanese sweet flag in the same way as the water lily, but place it in the barrel so that its roots sit 4" to 6" below the final water level.

5 Plant the pickerel weed as described above, and position in the barrel about 12" below the surface of the water. Place a bunch of parrot feather in the water unsecured, and carefully add water to the barrel to fill.

A Pickerel weed (*Pontederia cordata*). Large, arrow-shaped leaves accompany spikes of starry blue-purple flowers in summer and fall on this aquatic plant.

B Parrot feather (*Myriophyllum aquaticum*). This floater has 4"-long stems bearing feathery dark green leaves. It is included as an oxygenating plant to help keep the water clear.

C Variegated Japanese sweet flag

(*Acorus calamus* 'Variegatus'). The slender, grassy leaves of this common water plant are striped in green and white, and grow 8" to 12" tall.

D Hardy water lily (*Nymphaea* 'Helvola'). The open, sunny yellow flowers and familiar olive green leaves of this plant are quintessential water garden features.

design maintenance

The simplicity of this garden and the durability of the plants included make caring for the design an easy task.

■ Fertilize with aquatic fertilizer tablets once a month during the growing season.

■ Remove all spent flowers and leaves from the lily over the season.

■ In cold-weather regions, after the first frost lift the plants, trim off the foliage, and store the roots in plastic bags in boxes, in a cool, frost-free location. If you've added fish such as koi, bring them inside.

- ALL ZONES
- FULL SUN
- LIGHT WATERING
- WINTER

creating your design

1 Make sure your plant stand is secure and won't tip over under the weight of the plant pots. Line the planter with plastic.

2 Put pea gravel in the bottom of all pots, and cover with potting soil. Plant 1 amaryllis bulb in a 6" pot, being sure to place the growing tip up.

3 Plant 5 'Grand Soleil d'Or' bulbs evenly spaced in a 6" pot, and 5 'Cragford' in a similar pot.

4 Plant 2 hyacinth bulbs, 1 each in 4" pots; divide 20 crocus corms into 2 groups of 10 and plant in two 4" pots, spacing the corms evenly.

A Bright Winter Bulb Show

S pring may seem impossibly far away as your garden sleeps through the dead of winter, but you can create a faux-spring show indoors to add bright blooming color to holiday festivities. The secret is to trick some bulbs into thinking that winter is past! The bulb species selected here are all easy to force and will reward you with a spectacular focal point in your living room or other sunny site. And these flowers will offer lovely fragrances as an added bonus. This design uses a self-standing, rustic wood box, but you can use a simple window box on an interior windowsill or some other container that allows room for the bulbs in their pots. Regardless of the container, tuck in Spanish moss or sheet moss to camouflage the individual pots and give the display a more natural feel. After bloom time, replace the pots of bulbs with other flowering or foliage plants. The ferns and ivy can remain year round to display with other plants.

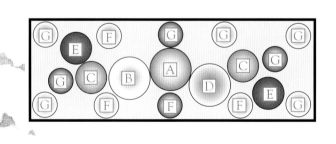

---

5 Plant 4 variegated table ferns singly in 3" pots; and 8 English ivies, each in a 3" pot.
6 Position all the pots in place in the planter and water well.

designguide

Bulbs can be forced in many innovative ways and containers and can even be unforgettable gifts. Consider forcing bright red early tulips in a wooden orange crate for a wonderful Valentine's Day present. Grow narcissus in a shallow bowl in pebbles in water, or netted iris in old coffee cups to bring a living, fragrant bouquet to the kitchen table.

A Amaryllis (*Hippeastrum* 'Orange Sovereign'). Zones 9-10. The large, brilliant orange trumpet flowers of this centerpiece tower over the other plants on 18" to 20" stems, set off by strap-shaped, dark green foliage.

B Narcissus (*Narcissus tazetta* 'Grand Soleil d'Or'). Zones 9-10. The bright, lemon yellow flowers of this cultivar have orange centers and grow on stems 12" to 14" tall. The flowers are sweetly fragrant.

C Hyacinth (*Hyacinthus* 'Delft Blue'). Zones 4-8. These Easter

favorites offer 6"- to 8"-tall, dense spikes of fragrant delphinium-blue flowers. Just one can fill a large room with a wonderful perfume.

D Narcissus (*Narcissus tazetta* 'Cragford'). Zones 9-10. Providing a strong accent to the design, each 12" to 14" stem carries 3 to 5 white flowers accented with red-orange cups. 'Cragford' is intensely fragrant.

E Crocus (*Crocus vernus* 'Flower Record'). Zones 4-8. This bulb makes up for its diminutive 4" to 6" height with striking deep purple goblets

surrounding orange stigmas.

F Variegated table fern (*Pteris cretica* 'Albolineata'). Zones 9-10. The slender, ribbon-like, fingered leaves of this fern grow 10" to 15" tall, with a white stripe down the center of each leaflet. The foliage acts as a foil for the bulb flowers.

G English ivy (*Hedera helix* 'Glacier'). Zones 5-10. Growing 9" tall, this ivy has dark green leaves marked with white, on trailing stems that soften the edges of the container as they spill over the sides.

design maintenance

Most of the work for this design will come after the blooms have faded.

▪ After bloom time, keep hyacinth and crocus pots in full light, and water and feed routinely. When the leaves have yellowed, remove and keep the soil dry until planting time. Discard the bulbs of 'Cragford' and 'Grand Soleil d'Or', except in zone 7, where they can be planted out.

▪ In summer, set amaryllis pot outside in shade to allow the bulb to build strength for next year's bloom.

- ZONES 5-9
- FULL SUN
- LIGHT WATERING
- SUMMER

creating your design

1 Cover the drainage holes in a 24"-diameter pot with screening, and do the same with four 12"-diameter pots. Fill the bottom of each pot with 1" of gravel for increased drainage.

2 Fill the pots with free-draining potting soil. Plant 1 pineapple sage in the center of the large pot, and 1 purple basil, 1 creeping rosemary, 1 lavender, 1 chocolate mint geranium, and 1 golden lemon thyme spaced evenly around the edge of the pot. Plant 1 pot marigold on either side of the

Magnificent Herbal Tea Garden

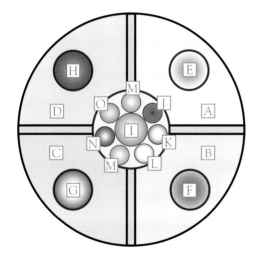

Store-bought tea pales in comparison to freshly brewed herbal varieties. This remarkable circle of herbs not only provides a bounty for the teapot, it offers a treat for all the senses. This design takes advantage of the fact that most herbs require relatively little space to grow and thrive. The combination of plants used here was chosen to give a wide range of tea flavors, but many of these herbs also offer wonderful fragrances and vivid blooms, not to mention a multitude of other culinary uses. Some of the plants selected benefit our well-being too: several have documented health benefits, from the calming effects of lavender, to the digestive relief and invigoration provided by peppermint. All do best in full sun, with average, well-drained soil. Harvest your "crop" regularly to keep the plants bushy and compact so that they won't encroach on their neighbors. Apply a liquid, balanced fertilizer at half strength monthly. Mix and match with other herbs to suit your own personal preferences.

pineapple sage, tucked among the other plants.

3 Plant the 4 smaller pots with curly spearmint, lemon balm, peppermint, and pineapple mint.

4 Plant 1 design quarter with 12 wild strawberries, 8" apart. Plant another with 5 variegated common thyme, 18" apart. Plant the third quarter with 8 German chamomile plants, 18" apart.

5 After putting the pots in position, plant the final quarter with 8 sweet woodruff, 12" apart. Water the entire design well, ensuring that the soil in the pots is well soaked.

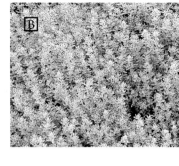

A Wild strawberry (*Fragaria vesca*). Zones 4-8. Featuring distinctive three-part, fan-shaped leaves, this perennial offers small white flowers followed by pea-sized seedy fruits. The leaves make a fruity tea.

B Variegated common thyme (*Thymus vulgaris* 'Silver Queen'). Zones 5-8. Growing 6" to 10" tall, this herb has tiny evergreen leaves edged with silver, and pale mauve flowers. Brew the leaves for a spicy, pungent tea.

C Sweet woodruff (*Galium odoratum*). Zones 3-9. The attractive starry whorls of foliage on this herb are topped with clusters of tiny white flowers in May. The dried leaves make a nice woodsy tea.

D German chamomile (*Matricaria recutita*). Zones 4-8. White daisy flowerheads top 1'- to 2'-tall ferny foliage on this herb. The flowerheads are used to brew a mild, relaxing, apple-like tea.

E Lemon balm (*Melissa officinalis* 'Aurea'). Zones 4-9. This hardy perennial grows 1' to 2' tall, with yellow variegated, mint-like foliage. The lemon-scented leaves make a refreshing hot or iced tea.

F Pineapple mint (*Mentha suaveolens* 'Variegata'). Zones 7-9. The wrinkled, woolly leaves on this 1'- to 2'-tall herb are edged in cream. Although not as robust as other mints, the tea from the leaves is delicious hot or cold.

G Curly spearmint (*Mentha spicata* 'Crispa'). Zones 4-9. The crinkle-edged, bright green foliage of this herb grows 1' to 2' tall. The leaves make a strong, minty tea that is used to aid digestion.

H Peppermint (*Mentha* x *piperita*). Zones 4-9. This 2'-tall herb features square stems that carry opposite-toothed, lance-shaped leaves, and clusters of mauve flowers along the stem. The leaves make a stimulating tea that's soothing to the digestive system and alleviates bad breath.

I Pineapple sage (*Salvia elegans*). Zones 8-10. Growing 3' tall, the pineapple-scented, bright green foliage can make quite an impression. Loose spikes of two-lipped scarlet flowers appear in fall. Leaves make a pineapple-melon-flavored tea.

J Purple basil (*Ocimum basilicum* 'Purple Ruffles'). This annual has purple-black leaves and clusters of pink flowers along the stem. It grows 18" to 2' tall; pinch to increase bushiness. The leaves and flowers make an attractive pinkish tea with mild peppery clove overtones.

K Creeping rosemary (*Rosmarinus officinalis* 'Prostratus'). Zones 8-10. A trailing cultivar that grows 6" to 12" tall, this herb has gray-green needle-like leaves and pale blue flowers. Use either to brew a piney tea.

L Chocolate mint geranium (*Pelargonium tomentosum* 'Chocolate Mint'). Zones 10-11. This geranium

grows 1' tall with velvety gray-green leaves marked with chocolate spots, and small, star-shaped white flowers. Make a minty tea from the foliage.

M Pot marigold (*Calendula officinalis*). This annual reaches 18" tall with mid-green foliage and small, bright orange flowers. Use the petals or the whole flowers to make a slightly bitter tea.

N Lavender (*Lavandula angustifolia*). Zones 5-8. This 1'- to 2'-tall scented favorite sends up spikes of purple flowers. The grey-green leaves carry the scent, but the flowers make a delicious pale green tea with mild floral overtones.

O Golden lemon thyme (*Thymus* x *citriodorus* 'Aurea'). Zones 5-8. This plant grows 6" to 8" tall, and has trailing stems with pungent, small, gold-rimmed leaves and tiny pinkish flowers. The leaves make a spicy tea.

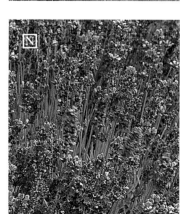

Design Alternatives

A Fence in Full Bloom

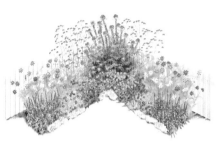

A Spider flower (*Cleome hassleriana* 'Violet Queen')
B Flowering tobacco (*Nicotiana alata* Nicki hybrids)
C Tall verbena (*Verbena bonariensis*)
D California poppy (*Eschscholzia californica* Thai Silk series)
E Cosmos (*Cosmos bipinnatus* Sea Shells mix)
F Mealy-cup sage (*Salvia farinacea* 'Victoria')
G Sweet alyssum (*Lobularia maritima* 'Rosie O'Day')

A Pincushion flower (*Scabiosa caucasica* 'Fama')
B Four o' clocks (*Mirabilis jalapa*)
C Yarrow (*Achillea millefolium* 'Cerise Queen')
D Indian mallow (*Abutilon* Summer Sherbert mix)
E Painted daisy (*Chrysanthemum carinatum*)
F Catmint (*Nepeta x faassenii*)
G Floss flower (*Ageratum houstonianum*)

Brilliant Color for a Shady Corner

A Rosebay rhododendron (*Rhododendron maximum*)
B Variegated Solomon's seal (*Polygonatum odoratum* 'Variegatum')
C Astilbe (*Astilbe x arendsii* 'Cattleya')
D Astilbe (*Astilbe thunbergii* 'Bressingham Beauty')
E Barrenwort (*Epimedium x rubrum*)
F Sweet woodruff (*Galium odoratum*)
G Christmas fern (*Polystichum acrostichoides*)
H Bethlehem sage (*Pulmonaria saccharata* 'Mrs. Moon')
I White foxglove (*Digitalis purpurea* 'Alba')

A Roseshell azalea (*Rhododendron prinophyllum*)
B Spike gayfeather (*Liatris spicata* 'Alba')
C Goatsbeard (*Aruncus dioicus*)
D Bergenia (*Bergenia cordifolia*)
E Bugleweed (*Ajuga reptans*)
F Mazus reptans 'Albus'
G Snowy woodrush (*Luzula nivea*)
H Hosta (*Hosta* 'Paul's Glory')
I Perennial honesty (*Lunaria rediva*)

Special Delivery

A Thread-leaf coreopsis (*Coreopsis verticillata* 'Zagreb')
B Daylily (*Hemerocallis* 'Black-Eyed Stella')
C Sweet autumn clematis (*Clematis terniflora*)
D Clematis (*Clematis* 'Multi Blue')
E Pincushion flower (*Scabiosa columbaria* 'Butterfly Blue')
F Blue oat grass (*Helictotrichon sempervirens*)
G Salvia (*Salvia x sylvestris* 'Blue Hill')
H Coreopsis (*Coreopsis* 'Flying Saucers')
I Veronica (*Veronica* 'Goodness Grows')

A Sneezeweed (*Helenium* 'Butterpat')
B Daylily (*Hemerocallis* 'Stella d'Oro')
C Rose (*Rosa* 'Climbing Orange Sunblaze')
D Morning glory (*Ipomoea tricolor* 'Heavenly Blue')
E Coreopsis (*Coreopsis grandiflora* 'Early Sunrise')
F Amethyst fescue (*Festuca amethystina*)
G Balloon flower (*Platycodon grandiflorus*)
H Heliopsis (*Heliopsis* 'Summer Sun')
I Salvia (*Salvia x sylvestris* 'Blue Hill')

Design Alternatives

A Bounty of Bark Color

A Scarlet willow (*Salix alba* 'Britzensis')
B Harry Lauder's walking stick (*Corylus avellana* 'Contorta')
C Golden willow (*Salix alba* 'Vitellina')
D Siberian dogwood (*Cornus alba* 'Sibirica')
E Wintercreeper (*Euonymus fortunei* 'Ivory Jade')
F Setterwort (*Helleborus foetidus*)
G White deadnettle (*Lamium maculatum* 'White Nancy')

A Variegated Tatarian dogwood (*Cornus alba* 'Elegantissima')
B Paperbark maple (*Acer griseum*)
C Yellowstem dogwood (*Cornus sericea* 'Flaviramea')
D Chinese witch hazel (*Hamamelis mollis*)
E Masterwort (*Astrantia major* 'Rubra')
F Cushion spurge (*Euphorbia polychroma* 'Emerald Jade')
G Sweet woodruff (*Galium odoratum*)

Splendor Among the Cracks

A Lady's mantle (*Alchemilla mollis*)
B Carpathian bellflower (*Campanula carpatica* 'Blue Clips')
C Cheddar pink (*Dianthus gratianopolitanus* 'Fire Witch')
D Myrtle spurge (*Euphorbia myrsinites*)
E Yellow corydalis (*Corydalis lutea*)
F Woolly thyme (*Thymus pseudolanuginosus*)

A Yellow saxifrage (*Saxifraga aizoides*)
B Moss phlox (*Phlox subulata* 'Blue Emerald')
C Gentian (*Gentiana alpina*)
D Snow-in-summer (*Cerastium tomentosum*)
E Dalmatian bellflower (*Campanula portenschlagiana*)
F Alpine campion (*Lychnis alpina*)

Flowerful Foundation Planting

A Purple-leaf sand cherry (*Prunus x cistena*)
B Rhododendron (*Rhododendron yakushimanum*)
C Oakleaf hydrangea (*Hydrangea quercifolia*)
D Variegated Japanese andromeda (*Pieris japonica* 'Variegata')
E Inkberry holly (*Ilex glabra* 'Compacta')
F Pincushion flower (*Scabiosa columbaria* 'Butterfly Blue')
G Butterfly bush (*Buddleia davidii* 'Nanho Purple')
H Columbine (*Aquilegia* hybrids)
I Bleeding heart (*Dicentra spectabilis*)

A Japanese maple (*Acer palmatum*)
B Mountain laurel (*Kalmia latifolia* 'Elf')
C White spirea (*Spiraea albiflora*)
D Japanese euonymus (*Euonymus japonicus* 'Albomarginatus')
E Boxwood (*Buxus sempervirens*)
F Milky bellflower (*Campanula lactiflora*)
G Chaste tree (*Vitex agnus-castus*)
H Coral bells (*Heuchera* 'Raspberry Regal')
I Penstemon (*Penstemon digitalis*)

Design Alternatives

A Hot-Hued Bed

A Lamb's ears (*Stachys byzantina* 'Helene von Stein')

B Daylily (*Hemerocallis* 'Stella d'Oro') C Sneezeweed (*Helenium* 'Moerheim Beauty')

D Veronica (*Veronica* 'Sunny Border Blue') E French marigold (*Tagetes* 'Queen Sophia')

F Verbena (*Verbena* 'Homestead Purple') G Black-eyed Susan (*Rudbeckia fulgida* 'Goldsturm')

H Daylily (*Hemerocallis* 'James Marsh')

I Thread-leaf tickseed (*Coreopsis verticillata* 'Zagreb') J Salvia (*Salvia x sylvestris* 'May Night') K Balloon flower (*Platycodon grandiflorus* 'Mariesii')

L Mexican zinnia (*Zinnia angustifolia* 'Golden Orange')

M Beebalm (*Monarda* 'Gardenview Scarlet')

N Butterfly weed (*Asclepias tuberosa* 'Gay Butterflies')

A Dusty Miller (*Artemisia stellerana*) B Yellow flag (*Iris pseudacorus*)

C Heliopsis (*Heliopsis* 'Summer Sun')

D Peach-leaved bellflower (*Campanula persicifolia* 'Telham Beauty')

E Coreopsis (*Coreopsis grandiflora* 'Robin') F Bush violet (*Browallia speciosa*) G Blanket flower (*Gaillardia x grandiflora*) H Crocosmia (*Crocosmia* 'Lucifer') I Blanket flower (*Gaillardia* 'Goblin') J Spike speedwell (*Veronica spicata* 'Blue Peter') K Milky bellflower (*Campanula lactifolia*) L French marigold (*Tagetes Bonanza series*)

M Four o' clocks (*Mirabilis jalapa*)

N Zinnia (*Zinnia* 'Cut and Come Again')

A Fall Decorating Garden

A Japanese silver grass (*Miscanthus sinensis* 'Adagio')

B European cranberrybush (*Viburnum opulus* 'Compactum')

C Dwarf hydrangea (*Hydrangea macrophylla* 'Forever Pink')

D Chinese lantern plant (*Physalis alkekengi*)

E Fountain grass (*Pennisetum alopecuroides* 'Hameln')

F Mini-pumpkin (*Cucurbita* 'Baby Boo')

G Mini-pumpkin (*Cucurbita* 'Jack Be Little')

H Gourd (Small Fancy Gourds mix)

I Ornamental pepper (*Capsicum annuum* 'Fiesta')

A Little bluestem (*Schizachyrium scoparium*)

B Holly (*Ilex*)

C Redvein enkianthus (*Enkianthus campanulatus*)

D Strawflower (*Helichrysum bracteatum*)

E Lilyturf (*Liriope muscari*)

F Rose (*Rosa* 'William Baffin')

G Blue passionflower (*Passiflora caerulea*)

H Sweet autumn clematis (*Clematis terniflora*)

I Globe amaranth (*Gomphrena* 'Strawberry Fields')

A Cool-Weather, Formal Vegetable Garden

A Snow peas (*Pisum sativum*)

B Snap peas (*Pisum sativum*)

C Fava, or broad, beans (*Vicia faba*)

D Beets (*Beta vulgaris*) E Red-leaf lettuce (*Lactuca sativa*)

F Green-leaf lettuce (*Lactuca sativa*)

G Kale (*Brassica oleracea*) H Spinach (*Brassica perviridis*)

I Broccoli (*Brassica oleracea*)

J Cabbage (*Brassica oleracea*)

K Swiss chard (*Beta vulgaris*) L Carrot (*Daucus carota*)

M Mesclun N Chives (*Allium schoenoprasum*)

O Parsley (*Petroselinum crispum*) P Violets (*Viola cornuta*)

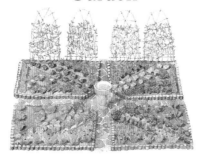

A Cucumber (*Cucumis sativus* 'Jazzer')

B Scarlet runner bean (*Phaseolus coccineus* 'Butler')

C Lima bean (*Phaseolus lunatus*) D Brussels sprouts (*Brassica oleracea*) E Garden cress (*Lepidium sativum*) F Endive (*Cichorium endivia* 'Neos') G Celery (*Apium graveolens* 'Green Giant') H Arugula (*Eruca sativa*) I White cauliflower (*Brassica oleracea*) J Cardoon (*Cynara cardunculus*) K Collard (*Brassica oleracea*) L Radish (*Raphanus sativus*) M Miner's lettuce (*Montia perfoliata*) N Chicory (*Cichorium intybus*) O Sweet marjoram (*Origanum majoricum*) P Nasturtium (*Tropaeolum majus*)

Design Alternatives

Fabulous Fall Color Border

suggestedplanting

suggestedplanting

[A] Japanese anemone (*Anemone hupehensis* 'September Charm')
[B] Maiden grass (*Miscanthus sinensis* 'Morning Light')
[C] Chrysanthemum (*Chrysanthemum* 'Clara Curtis')
[D] Aster (*Aster novae-angliae* 'Purple Dome')
[E] Ornamental onion (*Allium thunbergii* 'Ozawa')
[F] Mexican bush sage (*Salvia leucantha*)
[G] Montauk daisy (*Nipponanthemum nipponicum*)
[H] Obedient plant (*Physostegia virginiana* 'Vivid')

alternativeplanting

[A] Rough goldenrod (*Solidago rugosa*)
[B] Hakone grass (*Hakonechloa macra* 'Aureola')
[C] Wild ageratum (*Eupatorium coelestinum*)
[D] Boltonia (*Boltonia asteroides* 'Pink Beauty')
[E] Lilyturf (*Liriope muscari*)
[F] Bush clover (*Lespedeza thunbergii*)
[G] Boltonia (*Boltonia asteroides* 'Snowbank')
[H] Calamint (*Calamintha nepeta*)

A Rainbow of Roses and Friends

suggestedplanting

[A] Rose (*Rosa* 'Climbing Iceberg')
[B] Clematis (*Clematis x jackmanni*)
[C] Rose (*Rosa* 'William Baffin') [D] Catmint (*Nepeta* 'Six Hills Giant')
[E] Rose (*Rosa* 'Ballerina') [F] Rose (*Rosa* 'Belinda')
[G] Rose (*Rosa* 'Trumpeter') [H] Rose (*Rosa* 'Buff Beauty')
[I] Rose (*Rosa* 'Cornelia') [J] Rose (*Rosa* 'Yvonne Rabier')
[K] Rose (*Rosa* 'Mary Rose')
[L] Foxglove (*Digitalis purpurea*)
[M] Milky bellflower (*Campanula lactiflora*)
[N] Masterwort (*Astrantia major* 'Rosensinfonie')
[O] Sedum (*Sedum* 'Frosty Morn')

alternativeplanting

[A] Rose (*Rosa* 'Golden Showers')
[B] Climbing hydrangea (*Hydrangea anomola*)
[C] Rose (*Rosa* 'New Dawn') [D] Russian sage (*Perovskia atriplicifolia*) [E] Rose (*Rosa* 'Getrude Jekyll') [F] Mountain laurel (*Kalmia latifolia*) [G] Rose (*Rosa* 'Playboy')
[H] Rose (*Rosa* 'Jens Munk') [I] Rose (*Rosa* 'Peace')
[J] Rose (*Rosa* 'The Fairy') [K] Rose (*Rosa* 'Zephirine Drouhin') [L] Mullein (*Verbascum bombyciferum*)
[M] Delphinium (*Delphinium grandiflorum* 'Blue Mirror')
[N] Beebalm (*Monarda* 'Jacob Cline')
[O] Variegated lilyturf (*Liriope muscari* 'Silvery Sunproof')

A Fairy Tale Cottage Garden

suggestedplanting

[A] Butterfly bush (*Buddleia davidii* 'Petite Indigo')
[B] Butterfly bush (*Buddleia davidii* 'Pink Delight')
[C] Butterfly bush (*Buddleia davidii* 'Nanho Purple') [D] Honeysuckle (*Lonicera x heckrottii*) [E] Love-in-a-mist (*Nigella damascena* 'Persian Jewels') [F] Parsley (*Petroselinum crispum*) [G] Chives (*Allium schoenoprasum*) [H] Tricolor sage (*Salvia officinalis* 'Tricolor')
[I] Pot marigold (*Calendula officinalis* Bon Bon hybrids)
[J] Larkspur (*Consolida ambigua*) [K] Garden phlox (*Phlox paniculata* 'David') [L] Garden phlox (*Phlox paniculata* 'Starfire')
[M] Garden phlox (*Phlox paniculata* 'Laura') [N] Hollyhock (*Alcea rosea* Perennial singles) [O] Lavender (*Lavandula angustifolia*)
[P] Morning glory (*Ipomoea* 'Heavenly Blue')

alternativeplanting

[A] Chaste tree (*Vitex agnus-castus*)
[B] Rose-of-Sharon (*Hibiscus syriacus* 'Aphrodite')
[C] Rose-of-Sharon (*Hibiscus syriacus* 'Minerva') [D] Rose (*Rosa* 'Aloha') [E] Balloon flower (*Platycodon grandiflorus* 'Sentimental Blue')
[F] Basil (*Ocimum basilicum*) [G] Scarlet sage (*Salvia spendens*)
[H] Golden creeping Jenny (*Lysimachia nummularia* 'Aurea')
[I] Blanket flower (*Gaillardia x grandiflora* 'Goblin')
[J] Lupine (*Lupinus* Popsicle hybrids) [K] Snapdragon (*Antirrhinum* 'Summer Carnival') [L] Jupiter's beard (*Centranthus ruber*)
[M] Musk mallow (*Malva moschata* 'Alba') [N] Prarie mallow (*Sidalcea malviflora*) [O] Dusty miller (*Artemisia* 'Powis Castle')
[P] Clematis (*Clematis x jackmanii* 'Superba')

Design Alternatives

A Beautiful Butterfly Garden

suggestedplanting

- A Butterfly bush (*Buddleia davidii* 'Petite Plum')
- B Butterfly bush (*Buddleia davidii* 'Petite Purple')
- C Blue beard (*Caryopteris x clandonensis* 'Blue Mist')
- D Lavender (*Lavandula angustifolia* 'Munstead')
- E Chives (*Allium schoenoprasum*)
- F Frickart's aster (*Aster x frickartii*)
- G Cheddar pinks (*Dianthus gratianopolitanus* 'Spotty')
- H Purple coneflower (*Echinacea purpurea* 'Magnus')
- I Hybrid fleabane (*Erigeron* 'Prosperity')
- J Hybrid fleabane (*Erigeron* 'Foerster's Darling')
- K Rockcress (*Arabis caucasica* 'Variegata')
- L Coral bells (*Heuchera* 'Raspberry Regal')
- M Stonecrop (*Sedum* 'Autumn Joy')
- N Sweet pepperbush (*Clethra alnifolia* 'Hummingbird')
- O Dense blazing star (*Liatris spicata* 'Kobold')

alternativeplanting

- A Common lilac (*Syringa vulgaris* 'Monge')
- B Sweet mock orange (*Philadelphus coronarius*)
- C Russian sage (*Perovskia atriplicifolia*)
- D Globe thistle (*Echinops bannaticus* 'Blue Globe')
- E Dianthus (*Dianthus x allwoodii* 'Alpinus')
- F Boltonia (*Boltonia asteroides* 'Pink Beauty')
- G Verbena (*Verbena* 'Homestead Purple')
- H Black-eyed Susan (*Rudbeckia fulgida* 'Goldsturm')
- I Mist flower (*Eupatorium maculatum*)
- J Butterfly weed (*Asclepias tuberosa* 'Gay Butterflies')
- K Hens-and-chicks (*Sempervivum tectorum*)
- L Lobelia (*Lobelia* 'Compliment Scarlet')
- M Sweet woodruff (*Galium odoratum*)
- N Azalea (*Rhododendron* 'Lemon Drop')
- O Veronica (*Veronica* 'Goodness Grows')

A Full Spring Bulb Show

suggestedplanting

- A Species crocus (*Crocus chrysanthus* 'Goldilocks')
- B Species crocus (*Crocus chrysanthus* 'Lady Killer')
- C Species crocus (*Crocus chrysanthus* 'Cream Beauty')
- D Crown imperial (*Fritillaria imperialis* 'Lutea')
- E Snowdrop (*Galanthus nivalis*)
- F Daffodil (*Narcissus* 'February Gold')
- G Greigii tulip (*Tulipa greigii* 'Red Riding Hood')
- H Siberian squill (*Scilla sibirica* 'Spring Beauty')
- I Lily-flowered tulip (*Tulipa* 'West Point')
- J Daffodil (*Narcissus* 'Mount Hood')
- K Daffodil (*Narcissus peoticus recurvus*)
- L Tulip (*Tulipa* 'Georgette')

alternativeplanting

- A Species crocus (*Crocus chrysanthus* 'Gypsy Girl')
- B Species crocus (*Crocus chrysanthus* 'Striped Beauty')
- C Glory-of-the-snow (*Chionodoxa luciliae*)
- D Tulip (*Tulipa* 'Mrs. John Scheepers')
- E Striped squill (*Puschkinia scilloides*)
- F Greek anemone (*Anemone blanda* 'White Splendour')
- G Tulip (*Tulipa* 'Brilliant Star')
- H Iris (*Iris reticulata* 'Purple Gem')
- I Parrot tulip (*Tulipa* 'Flaming Parrot')
- J Summer snowflake (*Leucojum aestivum*)
- K Winter aconite (*Eranthus cilicica*)
- L Hyacinth (*Hyacinthus* 'White Pearl')

A Fabulous Winterscape

suggestedplanting

- A Chinese witch hazel (*Hamamelis mollis*)
- B Sweet box (*Sarcococca hookerana* var. *humilis*)
- C Variegated Japanese andromeda (*Pieris japonica* 'Variegata')
- D Hinoki false cypress (*Chamaecyparis obtusa* 'Nana Gracilis')
- E Lenten rose (*Helleborus orientalis*)
- F Setterwort (*Helleborus foetidus*)
- G Snowdrop (*Galanthus nivalis*)
- H Winter aconite (*Eranthis hyemalis*)
- I Bigroot geranium (*Geranium macrorrhizum*)

alternativeplanting

- A Paperbark maple (*Acer griseum*)
- B Oregon grape holly (*Mahonia aquifolium* 'Compactum')
- C American holly (*Ilex opaca*)
- D Chinese juniper (*Juniperus chinensis* 'Hetzii')
- E Allegheny foamflower (*Tiarella cordifolia*)
- F Coral bells (*Heuchera micrantha* 'Palace Purple')
- G Species crocus (*Crocus chrysanthus* 'Cream Beauty')
- H Iris (*Iris histrioides* 'Major')
- I Sweet woodruff (*Galium odoratum*)

Design Alternatives

A Spectacular Cut-Flower Garden

suggestedplanting

- A Butterfly bush (*Buddleia davidii* 'Nanho Blue')
- B Nasturtium (*Tropaeolum* 'Whirleybird Cream')
- C Lisianthius (*Eustoma* Double Eagle mix)
- D Mealy-cup sage (*Salvia farinacea* 'Victoria')
- E Bells of Ireland (*Moluccella laevis*)
- F Cosmos (*Cosmos* Sonata Series)
- G Tall verbena (*Verbena bonariensis*)

alternativeplanting

- A Rose (*Rosa* 'Peace')
- B Marigold (*Tagetes* 'Naughty Marietta')
- C Zinnia (*Zinnia elegans* Radiant series)
- D Veronica (*Veronica spicata*)
- E Cushion spurge (*Euphorbia myrsinites*)
- F Zinnia (*Zinnia elegans* Sun Series)
- G Baby's breath (*Gypsophila elegans*)

A Blooming Welcome

suggestedplanting

- A Sea pink, or thrift (*Armeria maritima*)
- B Basket-of-gold (*Aurinia saxatilis*)
- C Perennial candytuft (*Iberis sempervirens*)
- D Dalmatian bellflower (*Campanula portenschlagiana*)
- E Alpine pinks (*Dianthus alpinus*)
- F Yellow corydalis (*Corydalis lutea*)
- G Coral bells (*Heuchera* 'Firefly')
- H Mother-of-thyme (*Thymus serpyllum*)
- I Moss phlox (*Phlox subulata* 'Blue Emerald')
- J Siberian squill (*Scilla sibirica*)
- K Gregii tulip (*Tulipa greigii* 'Red Riding Hood')
- L Triandrus daffodil (*Narcissus* 'Thalia')

alternativeplanting

- A Rockcress (*Arabis x arendsii* 'Spring Charm')
- B Snow-in-summer (*Cerastium tomentosum*)
- C Perennial baby's breath (*Gypsophila repens* 'Alba')
- D False rockcress (*Aubrieta deltoidea* 'Variegata')
- E Ice plant (*Delosperma cooperi* Harlequin mix)
- F Cushion spurge (*Euphorbia polychroma*)
- G Veronica (*Veronica* 'Sunny Border Blue')
- H Bugleweed (*Ajuga reptans*)
- I Aubrieta (*Aubrieta x cultorum*)
- J Spring pea (*Lathyrus vernus*)
- K Gladiolus (*Gladiolus communis* ssp. *byzantinus*)
- L Leopard's bane (*Doronicum cordatum*)

An Amazing Autumn Bed

suggestedplanting

- A Sweet autumn clematis (*Clematis terniflora*)
- B Clematis (*Clematis orientalis*)
- C Dwarf fothergilla (*Fothergilla gardenii*)
- D Purple beautyberry (*Callicarpa dichotoma*)
- E Blue leadwort (*Ceratostigma plumbaginoides*)
- F Variegated lilyturf (*Liriope muscari* 'Variegata')
- G Hardy begonia (*Begonia grandis*)
- H Ornamental onion (*Allium thunbergii* 'Ozawa')
- I Cinnamon fern (*Osmunda cinnamomea*)

alternativeplanting

- A Rose (*Rosa rugosa* 'Alba')
- B Boston ivy (*Parthenocissus tricuspidata*)
- C Giant hyssop (*Agastache rupestris*)
- D Highbush cranberry (*Viburnum trilobum* 'Compacta')
- E Chrysanthemum (*Chrysanthemum* 'Vampire')
- F Purple moor grass (*Molinia caerulea*)
- G Monkshood (*Aconitum* 'Bressingham Spire')
- H Chinese lantern plant (*Physalis alkekengi*)
- I Eulalia grass (*Miscanthus sinensis* 'Aureola')

A Brilliant Box of Blooms

A Cupflower (*Nierembergia hippomanica* var. *violacea* 'Purple Robe')
B Marigold (*Tagetes patula* 'Naughty Marietta')
C Nasturtium (*Tropaeolum* 'Strawberries & Cream')
D Nasturtium (*Tropaeolum* 'Moonlight')
E Licorice plant (*Helichrysum petiolare*)

A Petunia (*Petunia* 'Purple Wave')
B Mexican zinnia (*Zinnia angustifolia* 'Orange Star')
C Geranium (*Pelargonium* 'Merlot')
D Trailing lobelia (*Lobelia erinus*)
E English ivy (*Hedera helix*)

A Shapely Succulent Collection

A Jade tree (*Crassula ovata*)
B Hen-and-chicks (*Sempervivum tectorum*)
C Pussy ears (*Kalanchoe tomentosa*)
D Burro-tail stonecrop (*Sedum morganianum*)
E String-of-beads (*Senecio rowleyensis*)
F Spider houseleek (*Sempervivum arachnoideum*)
G Jellybean plant (*Sedum rubrotinctum*)

A Bush cactus (*Opuntia microdasys*)
B Thick plant (*Pachyphytum compactum*)
C *Argyroderma fissum*
D *Sedum cauticola*
E *Sedum obtusatum*
F *Gibbaeum album*
G *Graptopetalum paraguayense*

A Winter Indoor Herb Box

A Curly-leaved parsley (*Petroselinum crispum*)
B Flat-leaved, or Italian, parsley (*Petroselinum crispum*)
C Common thyme (*Thymus vulgaris*)
D Variegated lemon thyme (*Thymus x citriodorus*)
E Chives (*Allium schoenoprasum*)
F Tricolor sage (*Salvia officinalis* 'Tricolor')
G Purple sage (*Salvia officinalis* 'Purpurea')
H Rosemary (*Rosmarinus officinalis*)

A Chervil (*Anthriscus cerefolium*)
B French tarragon (*Artemesia dracunculus* var. *sativus*)
C Savory (*Satureja spicigera*)
D Oregano (*Origanum x majoricum*)
E Dill (*Anethum graveolens*)
F Cilantro (*Coriandrum sativum*)
G Bay (*Laurus nobilis*)
H Fennel (*Foeniculum vulgare*)

Design Alternatives

Indoor Festival of Flowers

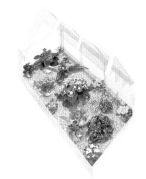

A   African violet (*Saintpaulia* hybid cultivars)
B   Miniature African violet (*Saintpaulia* hybrid cultivars)
C   Cape primrose (*Streptocarpus x hybridus* cultivars)
D   Cape primrose (*Streptocarpus x hybridus* small-flower cultivars)
E   Florist's gloxinia (*Sinningia speciosa* cultivar)

A   Moth orchid (*Phalaenopsis*)
B   Persian violet (*Exacum affine*)
C   *Serissa foetida*
D   Flamingo flower (*Anthurium scherzerianum*)
E   Cyclamen (*Cyclamen coum*)

Eye-catching Water Garden

A   Hardy water lily (*Nymphaea* 'Helvola')
B   Variegated sweet flag (*Acorus calamus* 'Variegatus')
C   Pickerel weed (*Pontederia cordata*)
D   Parrot feather (*Myriophyllum aquaticum*)

A   American lotus (*Nelumbo lutea*)
B   Umbrella plant (*Cyperus alternifolius*)
C   Miniature cattail (*Typha minima*)
D   Fanwort (*Cabomba caroliniana*)

Bright Winter Bulb Show

A   Amaryllis (*Hippeastrum* 'Orange Sovereign')
B   Narcissus (*Narcissus tazetta* 'Grand Soleil d'Or')
C   Narcissus (*Narcissus tazetta* 'Cragford')
D   Hyacinth (*Hyacinthus* 'Delft Blue')
E   Crocus (*Crocus vernus* 'Flower Record')
F   Variegated table fern (*Pteris cretica* 'Albolineata')
G   English ivy (*Hedera helix* 'Glacier')

A   Fritillaria (*Fritillaria meleagris*)
B   Lily (*Lilium* 'Santa Cruz')
C   Tulip (*Tulipa* 'Angelique')
D   Grape hyacinth (*Muscari armeniacum* 'Blue Spike')
E   Glory-of-the-snow (*Chionodoxa forbesii*)
F   Spider plant (*Chlorophytum comosum*)
G   Strawberry begonia (*Saxifraga stolonifera*)

suggestedplanting

Magnificent Herbal Tea Garden

A Wild strawberry (*Fragaria vesca*)

B Variegated common thyme (*Thymus vulgaris* 'Silver Queen')

C Sweet woodruff (*Galium odoratum*)

D German chamomile (*Matricaria recutita*)

E Lemon balm (*Melissa officinalis* 'Aurea')

F Pineapple mint (*Mentha suaveolens* 'Variegata')

G Curly spearmint (*Mentha spicata* 'Crispa')

H Peppermint (*Mentha* x *piperita*)

I Pineapple sage (*Salvia elegans*)

J Sweet basil (*Ocimum basilicum* 'Purple Ruffles')

K Creeping rosemary (*Rosmarinus officinalis* 'Prostratus')

L Chocolate mint geranium (*Pelargonium tomentosum* 'Chocolate Mint')

M Pot marigold (*Calendula officinalis*)

N Lavender (*Lavandula angustifolia*)

O Golden lemon thyme (*Thymus* x *citriodorus* 'Aurea')

alternativeplanting

A Feverfew (*Tanacetum parthenium*)

B Mugwort (*Artemisia vulgaris*)

C Caraway (*Carum carvi*)

D Pennyroyal (*Mentha pulegium*)

E Hyssop (*Hyssopus officinalis*)

F Russian comfrey (*Symphytum* x *uplandicum*)

G Betony (*Stachys officinalis*)

H Johny-jump-ups (*Viola tricolor*)

I Borago (*Borago officinalis*)

J Perilla (*Perilla frutescens*)

K Nasturtium (*Tropaeolum* Alaska series)

L Fennel (*Foeniculum vulgare*)

M Dill (*Anethum graveolens*)

N Coneflower (*Echinacea purpurea* 'Kim's Knee-High')

O Horehound (*Marrubium vulgare*)

Photo Credits

Opening Photos (pages 2-11)
Copyright: Dency Kane; Table of Contents: Lynn Karlin; Foreword: Dency Kane; Introduction: Marion Brenner

Modest Marvels Introduction (pages 12-13:
Allen Mandell

A Fence in Full Bloom (pages 14-17):
Illus.: Michelle Burchard; A, F, & G: Dency Kane; B, D & E: © 2001 Flora Graphic Inc.; C: Saxon Holt

Brilliant Color for a Shady Corner (pages 18-21):
Illus.: Grace Sharr; A: © 2001 Horticultural Photography; B, E & G: Dency Kane; C & H: © 2001 Flora Graphic Inc.; D: Pamela Harper; F: Ken Druse; I: Cathy Wilkinson Barash

Special Delivery (pages 22-25):
Illus.: Michelle Burchard; A & G: Alan & Linda Detrick; B:© 2001 Flora Graphic Inc.; C: Ken Meyer; D: Dency Kane; E & I: Courtesy of White Flower Farm; F: Michael Dreiza; H: Courtesy of Sunny Border Nurseries

A Bounty of Bark Color (pages 26-29):
Illus.: Michelle Burchard; A: Pamela Harper; B, C & G: Dency Kane; D: © 2001 Flora Graphic Inc.; E: Ken Druse; F: Courtesy of White Flower Farm

Splendor Among the Cracks (pages 30-33):
Illus.: Michelle Burchard; A, B & E: Courtesy of White Flower Farm; C: Joseph Strauch, Jr.; D: Lauren Springer; F: Cathy Wilkinson Barash

Flowerful Foundation Planting (pages 34-37):
Illus.: Michelle Burchard; A: Dency Kane; B: © 2001 Flora Graphic Inc.; C & D: Cathy Wilkinson Barash; E: Joseph De Sciose; F, G & H: Courtesy of White Flower Farm; I: Dency Kane

A Hot-Hued Bed (pages 38-41):
Illus.: Laura Vogel; A: Dency Kane; B: R. Todd Davis; C, D & H: © 2001 Flora Graphic Inc.; E & I: Alan & Linda Detrick; F, G & J: Courtesy of White Flower Farm; K: Cathy Wilkinson Barash; L: Rosalind Creasy; M: Richard Felber; N: Michael Dodge

A Fall Decorating Garden (pages 42-45):
Illus.: Michelle Burchard; A: © 2001 Flora Graphic Inc.; B: Andrew Lawson; C: © 2001 Horticultural Photography; D & E: Dency Kane; F: Keith Scott Morton; G: Dwight Kuhn; H: Lynn Karlin; I: David Cavagnaro

Grand Schemes Introduction (pages 46-47:
Hugh Palmer

A Formal Vegetable Garden (pages 48-51):
Illus.: Art Curtis; A, C, G, J, L, M & O: Rosalind Creasy; B, H & P: Cathy Wilkinson Barash; D & E & F: Dency Kane; G: Dency Kane; I & K: Lynn Karlin

Fabulous Fall Color Border (pages 52-55):
Illus.: Michelle Burchard; A: © 2001 Flora Graphic Inc.; B: Richard Shiell; C, F, G & H: Dency Kane; D: David Cavagnaro

A Rainbow of Roses and Friends (pages 56-59):
Illus.: Michelle Burchard; A, E, F, G & K: Dency Kane; B: Charles Mann; C: Courtesy of White Flower Farm; D & M: © 2001 Flora Graphic Inc.; H: Alan & Linda Detrick; I: Clive Nichols; J: Mike Schoup / Antique Rose Emporium; L: Keith Scott Morton; N: Cathy Wilkinson Barash; O: Ruth Rogers Clausen

A Fairy Tale Cottage Garden (pages 60-63):
Illus.: Michelle Burchard; A: Ken Meyer; B, C & P: Dency Kane; D & M: Alan & Linda Detrick; E, G, H & I: Rosalind Creasy; F: Cathy Wilkinson Barash; J: Charles Mann; K: Ken Druse; L: Bill Johnson; N: Courtesy of White Flower Farm; O: John Glover

A Beautiful Butterfly Garden (pages 64-67):
Illus.: Laura Vogel; A & N: Todd Davis; B: Ken Meyer; C, D, F, G, H & K: Dency Kane; E: David Cavagnaro; I: © 2001 Horticultural Photography; J: © 2001 Flora Graphic Inc.; L: Saxon Holt; M & O: Courtesy of White Flower Farm

A Full Spring Bulb Show (pages 68-71):
Illus.: Michelle Burchard; A: © 2001 Flora Graphic Inc.; B: Michael Dodge; C, D, F, G, I, J & K: Courtesy of Netherlands Flower Bulb Information Center; E & L: Dency Kane; H: Lauren Springer

A Fabulous Winterscape (pages 72-75):
Illus.: Michelle Burchard; A: Michael Dodge; B & F: © 2001 Flora Graphic Inc.; C, H & I: Dency Kane; D: David Cavagnaro; F: David McDonald; G: Courtesy of White Flower Farm

A Spectacular Cut-Flower Garden (pages 76-79):
Illus.: Michelle Burchard; A & D: Dency Kane; B & F: Rosalind Creasy; C: Lynn Karlin; E: David Cavagnaro; G: Saxon Holt

A Blooming Welcome (pages 80-83):
Illus.: Art Curtis; A: © 2001 Flora Graphic Inc.; B, C & L: Dency Kane; D: Alan & Linda Detrick; E: Charles Mann; F: Courtesy of White Flower Farm; G: © 2001 Horticultural Photography; H: Lynn Karlin; I: Ken Druse; J: Lauren Springer; K: Courtesy of Netherlands Flower Bulb Information Center

An Amazing Autumn Bed (pages 84-87):
Illus.: Michelle Burchard; A: Ken Meyer; B: Alan & Linda Detrick; C & E: Dency Kane; D & F: Courtesy of White Flower Farm; G: John Glover; H: Courtesy of White Flower Farm; I: © 2001 Flora Graphic Inc.

Stunning Containers Introduction (pages 88-89:
Dency Kane

A Brilliant Box of Blooms (pages 90-93):
Illus.: Michelle Burchard; A: David Cavagnaro; B: Bill Johnson; C: Rosalind Creasy; D: © 2001 Flora Graphic Inc.; E: Dency Kane

A Shapely Succulent Collection (pages 94-97):
Illus.: Michelle Burchard; A: Ken Druse; B: Rosalind Creasy; C: © 2001 Flora Graphic Inc.; D: Alan & Linda Detrick; E: Bill Johnson; F: Joseph De Sciose; G: Jerry Pavia

A Winter Indoor Herb Box (pages 98-101):
Illus.: Michelle Burchard; A, D, E & F: Rosalind Creasy; B, C & H: Dency Kane; G: Clive Nichols

Indoor festival of flowers (pages 102-105):
Illus.: Michelle Burchard; A, C & E: Alan & Linda Detrick; B: Ken Druse; D: Saxon Holt

Eye-catching Water Garden (pages 106-109):
Illus.: Michelle Burchard; A: Dency Kane; B: Alan & Linda Detrick; C: Gay Bumgarner; D: Ken Druse

Bright Winter Bulb Show (pages 110-113):
Illus.: Michelle Burchard; A: Courtesy of Netherlands Flower Bulb Information Center; B, C, D & F: © 2001 Flora Graphic Inc.; E: Ken Meyer; G: Ken Druse

Magnificent Herbal Tea Garden (pages 114-117):
Illus.: Michelle Burchard; A: Ken Druse; B, C, G, K & O: Rosalind Creasy; D, F, I & M: Dency Kane; E & J: © 2001 Flora Graphic Inc.; H: David Cavagnaro; L: Alan & Linda Detrick; N: John Glover

Resources

The Antique Rose Emporium
9300 Lueckemeyer Road
Brenham, TX 77833
(800) 441-0002; fax: (979) 836-0928
Web site: www.wearerose.com
Catalog: $5

W. Atlee Burpee & Co.
300 Park Ave.
Warminster, PA 18991-0001
(800) 888-1447; fax: (800) 487-5530
Web site: www.burpee.com
Catalog: Free

Bluestone Perennials
7211 Middle Ridge Road
Madison, OH 44057
(800) 852-5243 (phone and fax)
Web site:
www.bluestoneperennials.com
Catalog: Free

Breck's
6523 N. Galena Road
Peoria, IL 61632
(800) 806-1972; fax: (800) 340-7793
Web site: www.brecks.com
Catalog: Free

Brent & Becky's Bulbs
7463 Heath Trail
Gloucester, VA 23061
(804) 693-3966, fax: (804) 693-9436
Web site:
www.brentandbeckysbulbs.com
Catalog: Free

Busse Gardens
17160 245th Ave.
Big Lake, MN 55309
(800) 544-3192; fax: (763) 263-1473
Web site: www.bussegardens.com
Catalog: $3

Carroll Gardens, Inc.
444 E. Main Street
Westminster, MD 21157
(800) 638-6334; fax: (410) 857-4112
Web site: www.carrollgardens.com
Catalog: $3

Collector's Nursery
16804 N.E. 102 Ave.
Battle Ground, WA 98604
(360) 574-3832; fax: (360) 571-8540
Web site: www.collectorsnursery.com
Catalog: $2

Completely Clematis Specialty Nursery
271 Argilla Road
Ipswich, MA 01938
(978) 356-3197
Web site: www.clematisnursery.com
Catalog: Free

David Austin Roses, Ltd.
15393 Hwy. 64 West
Tyler, TX 75704
(800) 328-8893
Web site: www.davidaustinroses.com
Catalog: Free

Donovan's Roses
PO Box 37800
Shreveport, LA 71133
(318) 861-6693; fax: (318) 861-0670
E-mail: donovankas@aol.com
Free price list

Fox Hill Nursery
347 Lunt Road
Freeport, ME 04032
(207) 729-1511 (phone and fax)
Web site: www.lilacs.com
Catalog: $1

The Fragrant Path
PO Box 328
Fort Calhoun, NE 68023
Catalog: $2

Glasshouse Works
Church Street
PO Box 97
Stewart, OH 45778
(800) 837-2142; fax: (740) 662-2120
Web site: www.glasshouseworks.com
Catalog: $2

Greer Gardens
1280 Goodpasture Island Road
Eugene, OR 97401
(800) 548-0111; fax: (541) 686-0910
Web site: www.greergardens.com
Catalog: Free

Grigsby Cactus Gardens
2326-2354 Bella Vista Drive
Vista, CA 92084-7836
(760) 727-1323; fax: (760) 727-1578
Web site: www.cactusmall.com
Catalog: $2

Harris Seeds
355 Paul Road
PO Box 24966
Rochester, NY 14694-0966
(800) 514-4441; fax: (877) 892-9197
Web site: www.harrisseeds.com
Catalog: Free

Heronswood Nursery, Ltd.
7530 N.E. 288th Street
Kingston, WA 98346
(360) 297-4172; fax: (360) 297-8321
Web site: www.heronswood.com
Catalog: $5

High Country Gardens
2902 Rufina Street
Santa Fe, NM 87505
(800) 925-9387; fax: (800) 925-0097
Web site:
www.highcountrygardens.com
Catalog: Free

Jackson & Perkins
2518 South Pacific Hwy.
Medford, OR 97501
(800) 292-4769; fax: (800) 242-0329
Web site:
www.jacksonandperkins.com
Catalog: Free

Lowe's Roses
6 Sheffield Road
Nashua, NH 03062
(603) 888-2214; fax: (603) 888-6112
Web site: www.loweroses.com
Catalog: $3

Nichols Garden Nursery, Inc.
1190 Old Salem Road NE
Albany, OR 97321-4580
(541) 928-9280; fax: (800) 231-5306
Web site:
www.nicholsgardennursery.com
Catalog: Free

Oak Hill Gardens
PO Box 25
37W550 Binnie Road
Dundee, IL 60118
(847) 428-8500; fax: (847) 428-8527
Web site: oakhillgardens.com
Catalog: Free

Old House Gardens
536 Third Street
Ann Arbor, MI 48103
(734) 995-1486; fax: (734) 995-1687
Web site: www.oldhousegardens.com
Catalog: $2

Park Seed Co.
1 Parkton Ave.
Greenwood, SC 29647
(800) 845-3369; fax: (800) 275-9941
Web site: www.parkseed.com
Catalog: Free

Theodore Payne Foundation
10459 Tuxford Street
Sun Valley, CA 91352
(818) 768-1802; fax: (818) 768-5215
Web site: www.theodorepayne.org
Catalog: $3.50

Plant Delights Nursery, Inc.
9241 Sauls Road
Raleigh, NC 27603

Seeds of Change
PO Box 15700
Santa Fe, NM 87506-5700
(888) 213-0076; fax: (864) 329-4762
Web site: www.seedsofchange.com
Catalog: Free

John Scheepers, Inc.
23 Tulip Drive
Bantam, CT 06750
(860) 567-0838; fax: (860) 567-5323
Web site: wwwjohnscheepers.com
Catalog: Free

Select Seeds–Antique Flowers
180 Stickney Hill Road
Union, CT 06076-4617
(860) 684-9310; fax: (800) 653-3304
Web site: www.selectseeds.com
Catalog: Free

Sheffield's Seed Co., Inc.
237 Auburn Road
Locke, NY 13092
(315) 497-1058; fax: (315) 497-1059
Web site: www.sheffields.com
Catalog: Free

Thompson & Morgan, Inc.
PO Box 1308
Jackson, NJ 08527
(800) 274-7333; fax: (888) 466-4769
Web site:
www.thompson-morgan.com
Catalog: Free

Trans-Pacific Nursery
20110 Canyon Road
Sheridan, OR 97378
(503) 843-4214 (fax only)
Web site: www.worldplants.com.

André Viette Farm & Nursery
PO Box 1109
Fishersville, VA 22939
(540) 943-2315; fax: (540) 943-0782
Catalog: $5

Waterford Gardens
74 E. Allendale Road
Saddle River, NJ 07458
(201) 327-0721; fax: (201) 327-0684
Web site: www.waterford-gardens.com
Catalog: $5

Wayside Gardens
1 Garden Lane
Hodges, SC 29695
(800) 845-1124; fax: (800) 457-9712
Web site: www.waysidegardens.com
Catalog: Free

Well-Sweep Herb Farm
205 Mt. Bethel Road
Port Murray, NJ 07865
(908) 852-5390; fax: (908) 852-1649
Catalog: $2

White Flower Farm
PO Box 50
Litchfield, CT 06759-0050
(800) 503-9624; fax: (800) 496-1418
Web site: www.whiteflowerfarm.com
Catalog: Free

Woodside Gardens
1191 Egg & I Road
Chimacum, WA 98325
(800) 473-1152 (phone and fax)
Web site:
www.woodsidegardens.com

Woodlanders, Inc.
1128 Colleton Ave.
Aiken, SC 29801
(803) 648-7522 (fax also)
Web site: www.woodlanders.com
Catalog: $2

Yucca Do Nursery
Rt. 3, Box 104
Hempstead, TX 77445
(409) 826-4580
Catalog: $4

Major Display Gardens

Birmingham Botanical Gardens
2612 Lane Park Road
Birmingham, AL 35223
Web site: www.bbgardens.org

Eureka Springs Gardens
Rt. 6, Box 362
Eureka Springs, AR 72632
(501) 253-9256
Web site: www.eurekagardens.com

Desert Botanical Garden
1201 North Galvin Parkway
Phoenix, AZ 85008
(480) 941-1225
Web site: www.dbg.org

The Arboretum of Los Angeles
301 North Baldwin Ave.
Arcadia, CA 91007
(626) 821-3222
Web site: www.arboretum.org

Regional Parks Botanic Garden
Tilden Park
Berkeley, CA 94708
(415) 841-8732

Strybing Arboretum and Botanical Gardens
Ninth Ave. at Lincoln Way
San Francisco, CA 94122
(415) 661-1316
Web site: www.strybing.org

Denver Botanic Garden
1005 York Street
Denver, CO 80206
(720) 865-3500
Web site: www.botanicgardens.org

Audubon Fairchild Garden of the National Audubon Society
613 Riverside Road
Greenwich, CT 06831
(203) 831-1313

University of Delaware Botanic Garden
University of Delaware
251 B Townsend Hall
Newark, DE 19717
(302) 865-3500

United States Botanic Garden
245 First Street, S.W.
Washington, DC 20024
(202) 206-4083
Web site: www.nationalgarden.org

Fruit and Spice Park
24801 S. W. 187 Ave.
Homestead, FL 33031
(305) 247-5727

Atlanta Botanical Garden
1345 Piedmont Ave.
Atlanta, GA 30357
(404) 876-5859
Web site: www.atlantabotanicalgarden.org

Hawaii Tropical Botanical Garden
217-717 Old Mamalahoa Hwy.
Hilo, HI 96727
(808) 964-5233
Web site: www.htbg.com

Des Moines Botanical Center
909 East River Drive
Des Moines, IA 50316
(515) 283-4148

Idaho Botanical Garden
2355 Old Penitentiary Road
PO Box 2140
Boise, ID 83712
(208) 343-8649
www.idahobotanicalgarden.org

Chicago Botanic Garden
1000 Lake Cook Road
Glenco, IL 60022
(847) 835-5440
Web site: www.chicago-botanic.org

Washington Park Botanical Garden
2500 S. 11th Street
PO Box 5052
Springfield, IL 62705
(217) 544-1751
Web site: www.springfieldparks.com

Holcomb Botanical Garden
Butler University
4600 Sunset Ave.
Indianapolis, IN 46208
(317) 283-9413

Botanica, The Wichita Gardens
701 Amidon
Wichita, KS 67203
(316) 264-0448
Web site: www.botanica.com

Bernheim Arboretum
State Hwy. 245
Clermont, KY 40110
(502) 955-8512
Web site: www.bernheim.org

Laurens Henry Cohn, Sr., Memorial Garden
12056 Foster Road
Baton Rouge, LA 70895
(225) 775-1006

Brookside Gardens
1800 Glenallan Ave.
Wheaton, MD 20902
(301) 962-1404

Matthaei Botanical Gardens
University of Michigan
1800 North Dixboro Road
Ann Arbor, MI 48105
(313) 998-7061
Web site: www.isa.umich.edu/mbg

Minnesota Landscape Arboretum
3675 Arboretum Drive
PO Box 39
Chanhassen, MN 55317
(612) 443-2460
Web site: www.aboretum.umn.edu

Missouri Botanical Garden
4344 Shaw Blvd
St. Louis, MO 63166
(314) 577-5100
Web site: www.mobot.org

Crosby Arboretum
PO Box 1639
Picayune, MS 39466
(601) 799-2311

University Botanical Gardens at Asheville
151 W. T. Weaver Blvd.
Asheville, NC 28804
(828) 252-5190

International Peace Garden, Inc.
PO Box 116, Rt. 1
Dunseith, ND 58329
(701) 263-4390

Alice Abel Arboretum
Nebraska Wesleyan University
5000 St. Paul Ave.
Lincoln, NE 68504
(401) 465-2324

Rhododendron State Park
Division of Parks and Recreation
State of New Hampshire
172 Pembroke Road
PO Box 1856
Concord, NH 03302
(603) 532-8862

New Jersey Botanical Gardens at Skylands
PO Box 302
Ringwood, NJ 07456
(973) 962-7527
Web site: www.njskylandsgarden.org

Rio Grande Botanical Garden
2601 Central Ave. NW
Albuquerque, NM 87104
(505) 764-6200

Wilbur D. May Arboretum
Rancho San Rafael Park
1502 Washington Street
Reno, NV 89502
(702) 785-4153

Brooklyn Botanic Garden
1000 Washington Ave.
Brooklyn, NY 11225
(718) 623-7200
Web site: www.bbg.org

New York Botanical Garden
200th St. and Kazimiroff Blvd.
Bronx, NY 10458
(718) 817-8700
Web site: www.nybg.org

Toledo Botanical Garden
5403 Elmer Drive
Toledo, OH 43615
(419) 936-2986
Web site: www.toledogarden.org

Will Rogers Garden Exhibition Center
3400 NW 36
Oklahoma City, OK 73109
(405) 943-0827

Berry Botanic Garden
11505 S.W. Summerville Ave.
Portland, OR 97219
(503) 636-4112
Web site: www.berrybot.org

Henry Foundation for Botanical Research
801 Stoney Lane, Box 7
Gladwyne, PA 19035
(610) 525-2037

Longwood Gardens
Rt. 1, PO Box 501
Kennett Square, PA 19348
(610) 388-1000
Web site: www.longwoodgardens.org

Kalmia Gardens of Coker College
1624 W. Carolina Ave.
Hartsville, SC 29550
(843) 383-8145

Memphis Botanic Garden
750 Cherry Road
Memphis, TN 38117
(901) 685-1566
Web site: www.mephisbotanicgarden.com

Dallas Arboretum
8525 Garland Road
Dallas, TX 75218
(214) 327-8263
www.dallasarboretum.org

Fort Worth Botanical Garden
3220 Botanic Garden Blvd.
Fort Worth, TX 76107
(817) 871-7673

Red Butte Garden and State Arboretum of Utah
300 Wakara Way
Salt Lake City, UT 84108
(801) 581-4747

Lewis Ginter Botanical Gardens
1800 Lakeside Ave.
Richmond, VA 23228
(804) 262-9887
Web site: www.lewisginter.org

Bellevue Botanic Garden
12001 Main Street
Bellevue, WA 93005
(425) 452-2750
Web site: www.bellevuebotanical.org

Olbrich Botanical Gardens
3330 Atwood Ave.
Madison, WI 53704
(608) 246-4551
Web site: www.olbrich.org

Cheyenne Botanic Gardens
710 S. Lions Park Drive
Cheyenne, WY 82001
(307) 637-6458
Web site: www.botanic.org